THOMAS C[
AYRES & OBSE

THOMAS CAMPION

Ayres & Observations

Edited with an Introduction by
JOAN HART

Fyfield Books

First published in 1976
new edition 1989 by
Carcanet Press Limited
208-212 Corn Exchange Buildings
Manchester M4 3BQ

All rights reserved

Copyright © 1976, 1989 Dawson Jackson for the Estate of Joan Hart

British Library Cataloguing in Publication Data

Campion, Thomas
 Ayres & Observations. – (Fyfield books)
 I. Title II. Hart, Joan
 821'.1

ISBN 0-85635-100-8

The Publisher acknowledges financial assistance from
the Arts Council of Great Britain.

Printed in England by SRP Ltd, Exeter

CONTENTS

7   INTRODUCTION

    SELECTIONS FROM:
25 *A Booke of Ayres* (1601)
34 *Two Bookes of Ayres* (1613?)
52 *Third Booke of Ayres* (1617?)
63 *Fourth Booke of Ayres* (1617?)
73 'Poems and Sonets of Sundry Other Noblemen and Gentlemen' appended to Newman's edition of Sidney's *Astrophel and Stella* (1591)
76 *Observations in the Art of English Poesie* (1602)

90 Notes

91 Music for 'Author of light, revive my dying spright', from *Two Bookes of Ayres.*

93 Music for 'To Musicke bent is my retyred minde', from *Two Bookes of Ayres.*

94 Index of first lines.

INTRODUCTION

'Sweet Master Campion' — that contemporary epithet can hardly be bettered. Sweetness is Campion's keynote. Tempered variously by wit, mischief, melancholy and gravity, the sweetness never cloys. He himself rated the *Ayres* as 'superfluous blossomes of his deeper Studies'. Superfluous, to us, they are not; though 'blossomes' is apt enough.

Thomas Campion was born in London in 1567 'upon Ash Weddensday, and cristened at St. Andrewes Church, in Holbourne'. His father, 'John Campion, gent.', a clerk of the Court of Chancery, owner of property in Essex, and Vestryman of St Andrew's, died in 1576: the large sum of £50 was spent on his funeral. Within a year Thomas's mother married again. In 1580 she, too, died. At the age of fourteen, orphaned, he was sent by his stepfather to Peterhouse; and at seventeen he left Cambridge without taking a degree. A year later he entered Gray's Inn, presumably with the intention of following his father's profession. His name appears in 1588 amongst the performers in the Inn's 'Revels for the Entertainment of Lord Burghley', doubling as 'Hidaspes ye sonn' and — perhaps well cast after his much bereaved childhood — 'Melancholy'.

However, 'Content' was the pseudonym he chose for his first printed poems. Thomas Newman's 1591 edition of Sidney's *Astrophel and Stella* contained, amongst the added 'Poems and Sonets of Sundry Other Noblemen and Gentlemen', five 'Cantos' signed 'Content': the inclusion in Campion's first *Booke of Ayres* of one of these, 'Harke all you Ladies that doo sleepe', establishes them as his work. In both feeling and structure they show the influence of Sidney; 'What faire pompe have I spide of glittering Ladies', for instance, recalls the metre (though not the form) of 'O sweet woods the delight of solitarines' from *Arcadia*.

Those 'glittering Ladies', incidentally, sound as though they were dressed in stage costume; the behaviour of their knights would appear strange anywhere outside a theatre; in fact, the scene evoked must be part of a masque, of which only these cantos survived. This surmise is given substance by the fact that Campion is known to have contributed to the *Mountebanks Masque*, the *Gesta Graiorum* for 1594. Indeed Campion's first editor, A. H. Bullen, attributed to him the final song in that masque:

> The howers of sleepy night decaye apace,
> And now warme beds are fitter than this place.
> All time is longe that is unwilling spent;
> But howers are minitts when they yield content.
> The gathered flowers wee love, that breathe sweet sent;
> But loathe them, their sweet odours being spent:
> > It is a life is never ill,
> > To lye and sleep in roses still.
>
> The rarer pleasure is, it is more sweet;
> And friends are kindest when they seldome meet.
> Who would not heare the nightingale still singe;
> Or who grew ever weary of the Springe?
> The day must have her nighte, the Springe her fall;
> All is devided, none is lorde of all.
> > It were a most delightful thinge
> > To live in a perpetuall Springe.

This attribution is supported by the lyric's likeness to the 1591 'Canto 5'.

Campion's first acknowledged publication was a collection of Latin verses: *Thomae Campiani Poemata* (1595), comprising a minor epic about the defeat of the Armada; a long Ovidian fragment, 'Umbra'; elegies; and epigrams. Included were versions of two of the 1591 cantos. The author's own high estimate of his Latin compositions was shared by contemporaries: in 1598 Francis Meres mentioned him amongst those who 'have attained good report and honourable advancement in the Latin empyre'; and by his friend Charles Fitzgeffrey he was considered as second only to Sir Thomas More as an English writer of Latin epigrams. (William Covell, however, in *Polimanteia* (1595) tempered his praise with mild reproof for the extreme licentiousness of some of the poems.)

Little is known about Campion's life at this time. Despite the Gray's Inn connection, there is no evidence of his ever practising law. Indeed, his distaste for that profession may be judged from some of the Latin epigrams, and from the third stanza of 'Wise men patience never want' (published in 1613, but probably written much earlier):

> Kindnesse growne is, lately, colde,
> Conscience hath forgot her part:

> Blessed times were knowne of old,
> Long ere Law became an Art.
> Shame deterr'd, not Statutes then,
> Honest love was law to men.

How, then, did he support himself? In 1588 he had finally released his stepfather from all financial obligations except for the sum of £260 due to him under his mother's will.

In 1601, in collaboration with the lutenist Philip Rosseter, Campion published his first *Booke of Ayres*. Rosseter's dedication to Campion's patron, Sir Thomas Monson, makes it clear that only the first set of songs is by Campion: '. . . the first ranke of songs are of his own composition, made at his vacant houres' (vacant of *what*?) 'and privately emparted to his friends'. It is in this dedication that Rosseter tells us his collaborator 'neglects these light fruits as superfluous blossomes of his deeper Studies'. Whatever the 'deeper Studies' may have been (and Vivian's assumption that this and other references to them relate to the Latin poems is not wholly convincing), it is for the exquisite blending of words and music in this and in his subsequent *Bookes of Ayres* that Campion is valued today.

When the Campion-Rosseter *Booke of Ayres* appeared, the dominance of the Elizabethan madrigal had already been challenged by other composers. Dowland's *First Booke of Songs or Ayres*, for solo voice with instrumental accompaniment, had been published — with introductory Latin verses by Campion — in 1597. What distinguished Campion from other composers of solo songs was that he wrote his own words, as well as the music.

Whereas in madrigals the words were of secondary importance, often obscured by complicated polyphonic effects, lyrics written for the newly introduced fashion of solo singing had to fulfil strict poetic requirements. They were to be heard clearly: they had to be worth hearing. At the time when the English ayre flowered — briefly but abundantly — the music and the poetry were thus of equal importance. And, as poet-composer, Campion was well placed to take advantage of the time. While in his prose treatises he gave each of the arts in which he excelled a gentle nudge in the direction of its subsequent, separate development, in his published ayres he demonstrated repeatedly how happily words and notes could be united by one who was a master of both.

The music of Elizabethan and Jacobean songs had its roots in a long, still living, folk-song tradition; and when Shakespeare wrote songs for his plays he often fitted words to familiar melodies. In Campion's case, however, words and notes must often have taken form more or less simultaneously, interacting with and complementing one another. When one reads Campion's poems one experiences only half his creation — less than half, in fact: for the whole made by words and music is much greater than the sum of the parts.

A good example is a lyric from the *Divine and Morall Songs* — the one (for its musical setting see p. 93) which begins, 'To Musicke bent is my retyred minde.' These words are set to a gentle, expressive melody (in which there is, as often, a current of melancholy), that opens out for the next line: 'And faine would I some song of pleasure sing'. The completed melody is so pleasing that Campion repeats it — thus the next two lines of verse take their shape from it:

> But in vaine joyes no comfort now I finde:
> From heav'nly thoughts all true delight doth spring.

These words have been affected by the melancholy latent in the music. The poet discovers, in composing, that he is not after all in the mood for singing 'a song of pleasure', and the direction of the lyric has turned towards 'heav'nly thoughts'.

In the next line, 'Thy power O God, thy Mercies to record', with its hymn-like setting, both words and music ascend further heavenwards. The setting of the final line of the stanza, 'Will sweeten ev'ry note, and ev'ry word', is a kind of intensified reflection of the first line: formally satisfying and, fused with the words, a crystallisation of what has preceded it. Notes and words have both contributed and, successively, affected one another.

Finally, completing the binary form of the song, Campion repeats both music and words of the last two lines. This simple device, which he often used, works as a musical underlining, emphasising and strengthening the sense. Repetition of the words alone, without the music, would achieve the opposite effect — would dissipate the reader's attention. In this selection of the lyrics therefore, the repetitions, which have a purely musical function, have not been printed.

The words of Campion's *second* stanzas must, of course, always have been shaped to satisfy not only the demands of the chosen poetic form but also the musical requirements he had by then laid down. His placing of key words where the established musical phrasing requires them is usually skilful. Similarly, when the music composed for one lyric is used again for a later one (for example, the music he composed for 'Followe thy faire sunne' he later used for 'Seeke the Lord' with only slight changes in the melody — although the lute accompaniment was different), the words for the new lyric must, again, have been tailored to the notes.

Campion's next work to appear was his prose *Observations in the Art of English Poesie*, published in 1602. In its dedication he deprecates 'so simple a present, which, by some work drawn from my more serious studies I will hereafter endeavour to excuse'. The title page, though, makes large enough claims: 'Wherein it is demonstratively prooved, and by example confirmed, that the English toong will receive eight severall kinds of numbers, proper to it selfe, which are all in this booke set forth, and were never before this time by any man attempted.'

The reform of English prosody was something that had, before that time, been attempted by various men — by Ascham, Gascoigne, Harvey, Spenser, Sidney, and others. And Spenser had achieved it. By 1602 it should have been clear that English poetry was capable of standing on its own two feet and working by its own laws. What, then, induced Campion to revive the seemingly dead craze for classical 'numbers'? Sidney's argument that classical metres were more suitable for setting to music — more 'ayreable', to use Campion's own delightful term — may have appealed to him. The practice of *writing* in Latin had stimulated his interest in the subject; and 'these my late observations in English Poesy', although 'briefely gathered' for publication in 1602, are likely to have been formulated much earlier, when comparative chaos still reigned.

The *Observations* are presented *very* briefly: indeed, condensed sometimes to the point of obscurity. (Campion's habit of confining himself to essentials, based no doubt on his admiration for the pithiness of Martial's epigrams, may also owe something to his legal training.) In this treatise the author's reverence for the discipline of Greek and Latin forms prejudices him in favour of the use of classical metres, without, however, leading him to dismiss *all* native styles as 'barbarous': his constant aim is the enrichment of the poetic possibilities of English. If the dactyl is 'an attempt altogether against the nature of our language' (which few would deny), then the dactyl must go: the nature of English is what matters.

Another thing that, at least theoretically, must go is rhyme. Against that particular form of 'barbarism' he is adamant. Classical training had taught him that poetry was of divine origin; and what divinity was there in 'the rakehellye route of our ragged rymers ...

which without learning boste, without judgment jangle, without reason rage and fome' (as 'E. K.' put it in the Epistle Dedicatory to Spenser's *Shepheards Calendar*)? But Campion's case against rhyme, well-argued though it is, did not impress, for instance, Professor Saintsbury, who claims in his *History of Criticism* that all arguments against rhyme 'tell equally against Christianity, chivalry, the English constitution, the existence of America, gunpowder, glass-windows, coal-fires, and a very large number of other institutions of some usefulness'. Had the professor forgotten the celebrated note that, in 1669, Milton wrote on the verse of *Paradise Lost*? '. . . Rime being no necessary Adjunct or true Ornament of Poem or good Verse . . . but the Invention of a barbarous Age, to set off wretched matter and lame Meeter . . . a thing of it self, to all judicious eares, triveal and of no true musical delight; which consists only in apt Numbers, fit quantity of Syllables, and the sense variously drawn out from one verse into another, not in the jingling sound of like endings'. Between Campion and Milton, incidentally, there is more in common than the fact that both attacked rhyme. For example, Milton's practice follows Campion's theory in one technical particular: the occasional substitution at the beginning of a line of a trochee for an iamb.

In 1602, though, Campion had no such august support. And a refutation was soon published: Samuel Daniel's *A Defence of Ryme*. 'We could well have allowed of his numbers', says Daniel, 'had he not disgraced our Ryme, which both Custome and Nature doth most powerfully defend.' The unrhymed 'new numbers', moreover, do 'wrong to *England*, in seeking to lay reproach upon her native ornaments, and to turne the faire streame and full course of her accents into the shallow current of a lesse uncertaintie, cleane out of the way of her knowne delight.' But, paradoxically, he objects to the new 'eight severall kindes' of numbers as 'Onely what was our owne before, and the same but apparelled in forraine Titles, which had they come in their kinde and naturall attire of Ryme, wee should never have suspected that they affected to be other.'

Daniel's *Defence*, however, is eloquent and well reasoned. He makes one concession: 'my Adversary hath wrought this much upon me, that I think a Tragedie would indeede best comporte with a blank Verse'; but his panic about the idea of having to write without the assistance of rhyme obscures for him points of fundamental agreement with his 'unkinde [unnatural] adversarie': 'every Versifier', he says, 'that wel observes his worke, findes in our language, without all these unnecessary precepts, what numbers best fitte the Nature of her

Idiome' — failing to see that Campion's 'unnecessary precepts' were framed with the expressed intention of *helping* the search for those numbers that best fit the English idiom. Campion, though, may have considered that Daniel did *not* 'well observe' his own work: Ben Jonson, who told Drummond of Hawthornden that he had written a reply to both the *Observations* and the *Defence* (it has not survived), described Daniel as 'a good honest man, but no poet'.

Of course Campion (not alone amongst English poets in defying his own theory), did not in practice abandon rhyme. As Daniel said of him, his 'commendable Rymes, albeit now himselfe an enemy to ryme, have given heretofore to the world the best notice of his worth'; and so it was to continue. The complex internal rhymes of 'Ev'ry Dame affects good fame' might well have been contrived to demonstrate that he too, if he chose, could 'rime a man' (and a reader) 'to death'. There is about his attitude to rhyme something altogether perverse. His only song in Sapphics, 'Come let us sound with melody', is based, not on a classical model, but on a psalm; the rhymed lyric, 'The man of life upright', is freely adapted from a Horatian ode, *'Integer vitae scelerisque purus'*; and, significantly, when it came to reprinting one of these two in the *Divine and Morall Songs*, it was the rhymed example that he chose.

Both the attempt to discipline English verse according to classical rules, and the abjuration of rhyme, may have been wrong-headed: but both furthered Campion's poetic development. The search for new metrical patterns stimulated his natural rhythmic flexibility. His use of the caesura, 'the naturall breathing place' in a line, became even more subtle. The theoretical rejection of rhyme encouraged continual experiments with other devices — assonance, alliteration, half-rhyme, repetition, with the result that throughout the *Bookes of Ayres* rhyme appears simply as an additional grace.

Campion's search for new verse forms must seem particularly sympathetic to the modern reader. We are well placed to appreciate his skill, his ingenuity, and — his greatest strength — his impeccable ear for the cadences of his mother tongue. (In the Latin poems there are some ragged lines, without counterpart in the English lyrics: only in his native language could his ear for rhythm function properly.) For, notwithstanding his avowed preoccupation with metre, what governed his verse was the free, lively rhythm that he learned from Elizabethan music — a music full of irregular cadences, free from time signatures, its bars containing anything from four to fourteen beats. Despite the disciplines of writing in rhyme and of fitting words to music in successive stanzas, and despite the intricacy of his prosodic devices, Campion's lyrics have an astonishing freshness and ease; and because he has the rare gift of making the *unexpected* seem inevitable, his felicity hardly ever declines to facility.

At last Campion provided himself with the means of earning a living. In 1605, at the age of thirty-eight, he qualified in medicine at the University of Caen. His choice of a French university gives substance to the theory — based largely on evidence from the Latin poems — that in 1591 he had served briefly in the military expedition to Normandy led by the Earl of Essex.

In 1607 the *Masque in Honour of the Lord Hayes* was performed and published, 'Invented and set forth by Thomas Campion Doctor of Phisicke'. Limitations of space make it impossible in this volume to include material from the masques. In any case, although to Jacobean spectators every detail of the mythical or legendary plot, scenery and costume explained itself at once in the specific context of the performance, so much annotation is necessary for the modern reader that, in spite of Campion's lively and vivid prose descriptions, the printed page conveys at best a faint impression of what was, primarily, a spectacular musical entertainment.

An introductory poem to the *Hayes Masque* addressed to Theophilus Howard, Lord Walden, was Campion's first attempt to gain favour with the Howard family, protectors of his own patron, Sir Thomas Monson. In it he promises on behalf of his 'slender Muse':

> But if you favour her light tunes, ere long
> Sheele strive to raise you with a loftier song.

In 1613 Campion's *Lords Masque* was performed, celebrating the marriage of Princess Elizabeth to the Count Palatine. (The composer's fee was £66.13s.4d., Inigo Jones was paid £50 for his designs, and fifty-two performing musicians received £1 each.) Amongst the masquers were several members of the Howard family. Then, a few months later, that promise of Campion's was partly redeemed when Lord Walden's brother-in-law, Lord Knowles, presented the composer's *Entertainment at Caversham House*. The entertainment — sylvan rather than lofty — was designed for the amusement of Queen Anne who, suffering from the recent loss by marriage of her daughter Elizabeth, as well as from gout, was on her way to take the waters at Bath. On this occasion many Howards danced to Campion's tunes. Finally, at the end of the year, 'In the Banqueting roome at Whitehall, at the Mariage of the Right Honourable the Earle of Somerset and the right noble the Lady Frances Howard' (a great-grand-daughter of the poet Surrey), Campion paid his ultimate tribute to the Howard family.

This *Somerset Masque* was not designed by Inigo Jones, who was travelling in Italy at the time. Campion begins his description (published in 1614) by explaining: 'I grounded my whole Invention upon Inchauntments and several transformations. The work-manship whereof was undertaken by M. Constantine, an Italian, Architect to our late Prince Henry; but he, being too much of him selfe, and in no way to be drawne to impart his intentions, fayled so farre in the assurance he gave, that the mayne invention, even at the last cast, was of force drawne into a farre narrower compasse than was from the beginning intended. The description whereof, as it was performed, I will as briefely as I can deliver.' The Howards and other noble masquers were involved, it seems, in a fine backstage confusion.

1613, the year of the performance of the *Lords* and *Somerset* masques, is also the date of the *Songs of Mourning*, an elaborately organised sequence lamenting the death of Prince Henry, 'worded by Tho. Campion', with music by John Coperario. Probably the publication of Campion's *Two Bookes of Ayres*, containing the *Divine and Morall Songs* and *Light Conceits of Lovers*, should also be assigned to this year. Unlike the earlier and the later collections of *Ayres*, these songs are set out 'to be sung to the Lute and Viols, in two, three, and four Parts: or by one Voyce to an instrument': though the address 'To the Reader' says they were 'for the most part framed at first for one voyce with the Lute, or Violl'.

The publication date of *A New Way of Making Fowre Parts in Counter-point* is uncertain, but 1614 seems probable. Campion may have begun this treatise on music for his friend Coperario, who was music-master to Prince Charles. Later incorporated in Playford's *Introduction to the Skill of Musick*, it was reprinted several times, and in 1694 revised by Henry Purcell. The section 'Of Counterpoint' begins:

The parts of Musicke are in all but foure, howsoever some skilfull Musitions have composed songs of twenty, thirty, and forty parts: for be the parts never so many, they are but one of these foure in nature. The names of those foure parts are these. The *Base* which is the lowest part and foundation of the whole song: The *Tenor*, placed next above the *Base*, next above the *Tenor* the

Meane or *Counter-Tenor*, and in the highest place the *Treble*. These foure parts by the learned are said to resemble the foure Elements; the Base expresseth the true nature of the earth, who being the gravest and lowest of all the Elements, is as a foundation to the rest. The Tenor is likened to the water, the Meane to the Aire, and the Treble to the Fire. Moreover, by how much the water is more light than the earth, by so much is the Aire lighter than the water, and Fire than Aire: They have also in their native property every one place above the other, the lighter uppermost, the waightiest in the bottome. Having now demonstrated that there are in all but foure parts, and that the Base is the foundation of the other three, I assume that the true sight and judgement of the upper three must proceed from the lowest, which is the Base, and also I conclude that every part in nature doth affect his proper and naturall place as the elements doe.

True it is that the aunctient Musitions who entended their Musicke onely for the Church, tooke their sight from the Tenor, which was rather done out of necessity than any respect to the true nature of Musicke: for it was usual with them to have a Tenor as a Theame, to which they were compelled to adapt their other parts. But I will plainly convince by demonstration that contrary to some opinions, the Base contains in it both the Aire and true judgement of the Key, expressing how any man at the first sight may view in it all the other parts in their originall essence.

The sometimes almost scholastic way of expressing musical ideas which yet are far ahead of their time calls to mind Campion's attempt, in the *Observations*, to bring about a *new* kind of English verse by harking back to the precepts of antiquity. In the above passage, as in the *Observations*, Campion appears to make little distinction between demonstrating and stating; what he says, not three times, but just once, is evidently true. But the treatise does present original ideas, some of which were not developed by other musicians until many years later. He was the first English composer to maintain that the bass, rather than the tenor, 'is the foundation of the other parts'; he was the first to think clearly in vertical terms, to adumbrate the theory of chord progression; while his suggested simplification of the contemporary scale was a move in the direction of the modern octave. The section 'Of the Tones of Musicke' shows a sensitivity in the matter of key that was remarkable for his time:

> Of all things that belong to the making up of a Musition, the most necessary and usefull for him is the true knowledge of the Key or Moode, or Tone, for all signifie the same thing, with the closes belonging unto it, for there is no tune that can have any grace or sweetness, unlesse it be bounded within a proper key, without running into strange keyes which have no affinity with the aire of the song.

In one way, though, he was less original than he allowed himself to suppose. When he claimed that: 'If I should discover no more than this already deciphered of Counter-point, wherein the native order of foure parts with use of the Concords, is demonstratively expressed, might I be mine own Judge, I had effected more in Counter-point, than any man before me hath ever attempted', he must have conveniently forgotten that a similar theory of counterpoint had been expounded in 1597 in Morley's *Plaine and Easie Introduction to Practicall Musicke*.

In 1615 Campion was involved in the inquiry into the death in the Tower of Sir Thomas Overbury. On October 26th Campion confessed to having received, as an intermediary for his patron Sir Thomas Monson, the sum of £1400. His examiners apparently accepted his declaration that he did not know 'for what consideration it was pay'd'; and we must do the same. (Research has not yet confirmed the suggestion made by some writers of our own time — without indication of their sources — that Campion was imprisoned.) The £1400 was in fact payment for office, made — in accordance with standard Jacobean practice — by the newly-appointed Lieutenant of the Tower, Sir Jervis Elwes. Elwes was a pliant, credulous man: he did not know that his appointment had been engineered by Monson's protectors, the Howards, as a preliminary move in the plot against Overbury's life.

Monson, throughout his trial and imprisonment, denied complicity in the murder plot. Campion seems to have been convinced of his patron's innocence: that he attended him professionally in the Tower we know from the grant of official permission preserved in the State Papers, and from his own words:

> I, to whose trust and care you durst commit
> Your pined health, when arte despayr'd of it.

These lines come from the affectionate dedication 'To my honourable friend, Sir Thomas Mounson', which prefaces the *Third and Fourth Booke of Ayres* — published, after Monson's eventual pardon and release, probably in 1617.

In the *Third Booke* there are several sombre lyrics. One, beginning:

> O griefe, O spight, to see poor Vertue scorn'd,
> Truth far exil'd, False arte lov'd, Vice ador'd,
> Free Justice sold, worst causes best adorn'd . . .

surely refers to recent public events — to the injustice of the proceedings against Monson, and to the scandal surrounding Frances Howard and the Earl of Somerset, whose marriage had been celebrated in Campion's last masque. That event now appeared in an ugly light, for it was largely (the reasons are too complex to be explored here) in order to make the marriage possible that Overbury had been removed. Four minor figures in the sordid business (including Elwes) had been executed; Frances Howard had confessed her guilt; she and her husband had been imprisoned in the Tower, where Overbury had died.

Campion is not the only poet who may have felt at least a fool. For the Somerset marriage Ben Jonson had written two masques; Bacon had paid £2000 for the presentation at Gray's Inn of the deplorable *Masque of Flowers*; and in an 'Epithalamium' Donne had hailed the couple as 'Blest payre of Swans'.

In 'So tyr'd are all my thoughts' a more personal note is struck. The end of the third stanza,

> Poore I alone, dreaming, endure
> Griefe that knowes nor cause, nor cure

reminds us of that mysterious early lyric, 'The Sypres curten of the night', and renews our curiosity about the thoughts that tormented Campion's lonely nights.

In 1618 *The Ayres that were Sung and Played at Brougham Castle* (celebrating King James's return from Scotland) were published. Though the music was by George Mason and John Earsden, there is some evidence that Campion wrote the words. In 1619 an enlarged and revised edition of the *Poemata* appeared, with some of the salacities of the earlier edition toned down.

In the following year, on March 1st 1620, at the age of fifty-three, Campion died. He was buried at St. Dunstan's in the West on the same day. His will, made on the day of his death, bequeathed 'all that he had' to the lutenist Philip Rosseter, with whom he had produced his first *Booke of Ayres* in 1601. He 'wished that his estate had bin farr more'. The amount was £22.

Did he also wish that he had more to leave to posterity — some fruits, perhaps, of his mysterious 'deeper Studies'? His principal legacy to us is, of course, the *Ayres*. In assessing them it must be remembered that they were meant to be sung as well as read. When his lyrics appeared in contemporary verse miscellanies they would have been familiar to their readers already as *songs*. So completely did Campion achieve his aim of coupling 'Words and Notes lovingly together' that when we hear one of the ayres sung we find it almost impossible afterwards to read the words without recalling the music.

Since he wrote his lyrics not for the solitary reader but for groups of people making music, Campion was restricted to conventional subjects that could be treated simply and would be readily comprehensible: subjects from classical sources, or from the common stock of songbook material. His poetic innovations were in the treatment of the material, not in the material itself. The fact that he was composer as well as poet, however much it liberated his style, fettered his content.

The images are as conventional as the subject matter. Light and dark are contrasted, sun and shadow, fire and ice. There is about his lilies and roses, rubies and pearls, a slight smell of the theatre, as of exquisite properties designed by Inigo Jones for one of his masques. For example,

> Her rosie cheekes, her ever smiling eyes,
> Are Spheares and beds where Love in triumph lies:
> Her rubine lips, when they their pearle unlocke,
> Make them seeme as they did rise
> All out of one smooth Currall Rocke.

The next few lines, however, suggest an awareness that something was lacking:

> Oh that of other Creatures store I knew,
> More worthy and more rare:
> For these are old, and shee so new
> That her to them none should compare.

Though music, to a large extent, determined Campion's use of words, he also owed much to earlier English poets. He pays tributes to Chaucer both in an elegy in the 1595 *Poemata* and in the address 'To the Reader' at the beginning of the *Fourth Booke of Ayres*. 'Respect my faith, regard my service past' recalls Sydney, and Wyatt too; and the tones of both poets are often heard in his love songs. The climate of feeling of Sidney's *Astrophel and Stella* seems to have been particularly congenial to him (although he did not use the sonnet form). It is tempting to see the source of Campion's poems about sleeping women — the earliest, 'It fell on a sommer's day', is an English version of one of the 1595 Latin epigrams — in Sidney's

> Have I caught my heavenly jewel
> Teaching Sleep most fair to be?
> Now will I teach her that she,
> When she wakes is too too cruel.
>
> Since sweet Sleep her eyes hath charmed,
> The two onely darts of Love:
> Now will I with that Boy prove
> Some play while he is disarmed.

Campion also composed poems spoken by women. His contribution to the convention established by Wyatt and Surrey (and used by Sidney in.'My true love hath my heart and I have his') was to vary the personalities of the speakers: even the betrayed maidens are distinct one from another.

Not all his poems spoken by women are successful. 'If thou long'st to learn', for example, attempts an air of sophistication, but defeats itself. A masculine self-pity intrudes with the lines,

> Those sweet houres which wee had past
> Cal'd to minde, thy heart would burne

which fix our attention, not on the proud beauty who speaks them, but on her rejected lover; while the shortcomings of 'Faine would I wed a faire young man' exposed it to an anonymous parodist later in the seventeenth century, who, by changing a few words, made the speaker a man.

Most of the lyrics fall into four categories: laments for a mistress's unkindness (there are so many of these that the reader comes upon

'O, what unhop't for sweet supply' with a cry of relief akin to the writer's); devotional poems, which have often been undervalued; wittily wanton fancies; and grave, thoughtful, ironic expressions of tenderness, direct and shrewd. Sometimes we sense a poet who, if separated from the composer, might have written with more emotional complexity and breadth. Were music capable — as it is not — of expressing ambiguity, he might for example have considered in the same lyric the predicament of the supplicated mistress and the plight of the supplicating lover, instead of writing as he did separate poems embodying the two situations consecutively.

During his life Campion received much praise. As early as 1593 George Peele wrote of him, '. . . thou/That richly cloth'st conceits with well made words'; even Samuel Daniel saw him as 'a man of fair parts and good reputation'; and in 1605 William Camden included him (with Spenser, Jonson and Shakespeare) amongst the 'most pregnant witts of these times'. It is difficult to estimate how much effect he had on the work of his contemporaries. Do the lines:

> Now shew it, if thou be a woman right:
> Embrace, and kisse, and love me in despight

reveal the influence of Donne, or was Donne affected by Campion? Or was it a common tradition informing both? The *Divine and Morall Songs* were probably familiar to George Herbert, who was an enthusiastic lutenist. In the *Poemata* are two recurrent figures: Mellea, the mistress who responds too freely, and Caspia, who rebuffs. Restoration lyricists may be seen as developing the idea of Mellea, and Marvell, in 'To His Coy Mistress', as making the conclusive address to Caspia.

Campion devoted much time to revising his poems — invariably to good purpose. The process is clear in two versions of a poem, the first published in 1601, the second (with an almost identical vocal setting, but a new lute accompaniment), in 1617.

> Your faire lookes enflame my desire,
>   Quench it againe with love.
> Stay, O strive not still to retire,
>   Do not inhumane prove.
> If love may perswade
>   Loves pleasures deere denie not;
> Here is a silent grovie shade,
>   O tarrie then, and flie not.

Have I seaz'd my heavenly delight
    In this unhaunted grove?
Time shall now her furie requite
    With the revenge of love.
Then come, sweetest come,
    My lips with kisses gracing,
Here let us harbour all alone,
    Die, die in sweete embracing.

Will you now so timely depart,
    And not return againe?
Your sight lends such life to my hart
    That to depart is paine.
Feare yeelds no delay,
    Securenes helpeth pleasure:
Then till the time gives safer stay,
    O farewell my lives treasure!

(1601)

Your faire lookes urge my desire,
    Calme it, sweet, with love.
Stay, o why will you retire?
    Can you churlish prove?
If love may perswade,
    Loves pleasures deare deny not:
Here is a grove secur'd with shade,
    O then be wise and flye not.

Harke the Birds delighted sing,
    Yet our pleasure sleepes:
Wealth to none can profit bring,
    Which the miser keepes:
O come while we may
    Let's chayne Love with embraces,
Wee have not all times time to stay,
    Nor safety in all places.

What ill finde you now in this?
    Or who can complaine?
There is nothing done amisse,
    That breedes no man payne.

> 'Tis now flowry *May*,
>   But ev'n in cold *December*,
> When all these leaves are blowne away
>   This place shall I remember.
>
> *(1617)*

Even if we regret in the later version the loss of 'heere is a silent grovie shade', we cannot but see that the scene has been repainted in colours at once stronger and more subtle. The only lines common to both versions, 'If Love may perswade,/Loves pleasures deare deny not', are still placed where they provide an arresting change of metre. The shortening by a syllable of the first four lines of each stanza produces a fresh directness and simplicity — a simplicity unruffled by the new intricate patterning of the 'a' sounds of the remainder of stanza 2, or by the bold and affecting, 'Wee have not all times time to stay'. Campion's use of lines made up of monsyllables is always striking. And the early elegant clichés have given way to the sharpness of aphorism: 'Wealth to none can profit bring,/Which the miser keepes'; 'There is nothing done amisse,/That breedes no man payne'.

Above all, the later version is strengthened by the tension between the young man's experience and the older man's reflection upon it. The author of the 1601 version had not known December's recollection of May and could not have finished the poem so memorably.

What was Campion like? Occasionally a lyric suggests the personal; 'If any hath the heart to kill', for instance, appears convincingly to relate to an actual amorous event — or non-event. But such formal treatment of conventional subject matter does not tell us much about the author. We can only speculate. Let the lines which he addressed to a perhaps imaginary mistress stand as his epitaph:

> Thy voice is as an Eccho cleare, which Musicke doth beget:
> Thy speech is as an Oracle, which none can counterfeit:
> For thou alone without offending
> Hast obtain'd power of enchanting:
> And I could heare thee without ending,
> Other comfort never wanting.

Principles of Selection and Textual Notes

Most of this selection is taken from the *Bookes of Ayres*. The aim has been to print not only the best lyrics but also, with them, examples showing the author's range. Selections from the *Observations* illuminate some of Campion's techniques, and the verse illustrations (some of which would necessarily earn a place in any selection) gain from being read in context.

The text is based on the first editions (British Museum). The following emendations have been made: 'than' for 'then' (except where the rhyme would have been affected); 'pensive' for 'pensiue', and 'subject' for 'subiect'. The punctuation follows — as much as possible — that of the first editions. However, there are often discrepancies between the first stanza printed with the music and that of the full lyric printed lower on the page. Some commas have been added where clarity demands them but, in the interests of Campion's rhythm, as few as possible.

Reference has been made to the editions of Bullen (1903), Vivian (1909) and W. R. Davis (1969).

I should like to acknowledge the assistance given by the staff of the British Library.

Select Bibliography

Catherine Ing, *Elizabethan Lyrics* (London, 1951, 1968)
M. M. Kastendieck, *England's Musical Poet, Thomas Campion* (New York, 1938, 1963)
Edward Lowbury, *Thomas Campion, Poet, Composer, Physician* (London, 1970)
Thomas MacDonagh, *Thomas Campion and the Art of English Poetry* (Dublin, 1913)
Allardyce Nicoll, *Stuart Masques and the Renaissance Stage* (New York, 1938)
Bruce Pattison, *Music and Poetry of the English Renaissance* (London, 1948)

From *A Booke of Ayres* (1601)

To the Reader

What Epigrams are in Poetrie, the same are Ayres in musicke, then in their chiefe perfection when they are short and well seasoned. But to clogg a light song with a long Praeludium, is to corrupt the nature of it. Manie rests in Musicke were invented either for necessitie of the fuge, or granted as a harmonicall licence in songs of many parts: but in Ayres I find no use they have, unlesse it be to make a vulgar, and triviall modulation seeme to the ignorant strange, and to the judiciall tedious. A naked Ayre without guide, or prop, or colour but his owne, is easily censured of everie eare, and requires so much the more invention to make it please. And as Martiall *speakes in defence of his short Epigrams, so may I say in th' apologie of Ayres, that where there is a full volume, there can be no imputation of shortnes. The Lyricke Poets among the Greekes and Latines were first inventers of Ayres, tying themselves strictly to the number, and value of their sillables, of which sort you shall find here onely one song in Saphicke verse; the rest are after the fascion of the time, eare-pleasing rimes without Arte. The subject of them is for the most part amorous, and why not amorous songs, as well as amorous attires? Or why not new Ayres, as well as new fascions? For the Note and Tableture, if they satisfie the most, we have our desire, let expert masters please themselves with better. And if anie light error hath escaped us, the skilfull may easily correct it, the unskilfull will hardly perceive it. But there are some, who to appeare the more deepe, and singular in their judgement, will admit no Musicke but that which is long, intricate, bated with fuge, chaind with sincopation, and where the nature of everie word is precisely exprest in the Note, like the old exploided action in Comedies, when if they did pronounce* Memini, *they would point to the hinder part of their heads, if* Video, *put their finger in their eye. But such childish observing of words is altogether ridiculous, and we ought to maintaine as well in Notes, as in action a manly cariage, gracing no word, but that which is eminent, and emphaticall. Nevertheles, as in Poesie we give the preheminence to the Heroicall Poeme, so in Musicke we yeeld the chiefe place to the grave, and well invented Motet, but not to every harsh and dull confused Fantasie, where in multitude of points the Harmonie is quite drowned. Ayres have both their Art and pleasure, and I will conclude of them, as the Poet did in his censure, of* Catullus *the Lyricke, and* Vergil *the Heroicke writer:*

> Tantum magna suo debet Verona Catullo:
> Quantum parva suo Mantua Vergilio.

['As much as Verona owes to her Catullus, so much small Mantua owes to her Virgil.' Martial, *Epigrams XIV*.]

I

My sweetest Lesbia let us live and love,
And though the sager sort our deedes reprove,
Let us not way them: heav'ns great lampes doe dive
Into their west, and strait againe revive,
But soone as once set is our little light,
Then must we sleepe one ever-during night.

If all would lead their lives in love like mee,
Then bloudie swords and armour should not be,
No drum nor trumpet peaceful sleepes should move,
Unles alar'me came from the campe of love:
But fooles do live, and wast their little light,
And seeke with paine their ever-during night.

When timely death my life and fortune ends,
Let not my hearse be vext with mourning friends,
But let all lovers rich in triumph come,
And with sweet pastimes grace my happie tombe;
And Lesbia close up thou my little light,
And crowne with love my ever-during night.

II

Though you are yoong and I am olde,
Though your vaines hot and my bloud colde,
Though youth is moist and age is drie,
Yet embers live when flames doe die.

The tender graft is easely broke,
But who shall shake the sturdie Oke?
You are more fresh and faire than I,
Yet stubs do live when flowers doe die.

Thou that thy youth doest vainely boast,
Know buds are soonest nipt with frost,
Thinke that thy fortune still doth crie,
Thou foole, to-morrow thou must die.

III

I care not for these Ladies
That must be woode and praide,
Give me kind Amarillis
The wanton countrey maide;
Nature art disdaineth,
Her beautie is her owne;
   Her when we court and kisse,
   She cries, forsooth, let go!
   But when we come where comfort is
   She never will say no.

If I love Amarillis,
She gives me fruit and flowers,
But if we love these Ladies,
We must give golden showers,
Give them gold that sell love,
Give me the Nutbrowne lasse,
   Who when we court and kisse,
   She cries, forsooth, let go!
   But when we come where comfort is
   She never will say no.

These Ladies must have pillowes
And beds by strangers wrought,
Give me a Bower of willowes,
Of mosse and leaves unbought,
And fresh Amarillis,
With milke and honie fed,
   Who when we court and kisse,
   She cries, forsooth, let go!
   But when we come where comfort is
   She never will say no.

IV

Followe thy faire sunne, unhappy shaddowe,
Though thou be blacke as night
And she made all of light,
Yet follow thy faire sun, unhappie shaddowe.

Follow her whose light thy light depriveth,
Though here thou liv'st disgrac't,

And she in heaven is plac't,
Yet follow her whose light the world reviveth.

Follow those pure beames whose beautie burneth,
That so have scorched thee,
As thou still blacke must bee,
Til her kind beames thy black to brightnes turneth.

Follow her while yet her glorie shineth:
There comes a luckles night,
That will dim all her light,
And this the black unhappie shade devineth.

Follow still since so thy fates ordained;
The Sunne must have his shade,
Till both at once doe fade,
The Sun still proud, the shadow still disdained.

V

My love hath vowd hee will forsake mee
And I am alreadie sped.
Far other promise he did make me
When he had my maidenhead.
If such danger be in playing,
And sport must to earnest turne,
I will go no more a-maying.

Had I foreseene what is ensued,
And what now with paine I prove,
Unhappie then I had eschewed
This unkind event of love:
Maides foreknow their own undooing,
But feare naught till all is done,
When a man alone is wooing.

Dissembling wretch, to gaine thy pleasure,
What didst thou not vow and sweare?
So didst thou rob me of the treasure
Which so long I held so deare:
Now thou prov'st to me a stranger,
Such is the vile guise of men
When a woman is in danger.

That hart is neerest to misfortune
That will trust a fained toong;
When flattring men our loves importune,
They entend us deepest wrong:
If this shame of loves betraying
But this once I cleanely shun,
I will go no more a-maying.

VI

When to her lute Corrina sings,
Her voice revives the leaden stringes,
And doth in highest noates appeare
As any challeng'd eccho cleere;
But when she doth of mourning speake,
Ev'n with her sighes the strings do breake.

And as her lute doth live or die,
Led by her passion, so must I;
For when of pleasure she doth sing,
My thoughts enjoy a sodaine spring,
But if she doth of sorrow speake,
Ev'n from my hart the strings doe breake.

VIII

It fell on a sommers day
While sweete Bessie sleeping laie
In her bowre, on her bed,
Light with curtaines shadowed,
Jamy came: shee him spies,
Opning halfe her heavie eies.

Jamy stole in through the dore,
She lay slumbring as before,
Softly to her he drew neere,
She heard him, yet would not heare;
Bessie vow'd not to speake,
He resolv'd that dumpe to breake.

First a soft kisse he doth take,
She lay still, and would not wake;
Then his hands learn'd to woo,

She dreamp't not what he would doo,
But still slept, while he smild
To see love by sleepe beguild.

Jamy then began to play,
Bessie as one buried lay,
Gladly still through this sleight
Deceiv'd in her owne deceit;
And since this traunce begoon,
She sleepes ev'rie afternoone.

IX

The Sypres curten of the night is spread,
And over all a silent dewe is cast.
The weaker cares by sleepe are conquered,
But I alone, with hidious griefe agast,
In spite of Morpheus charmes a watch doe keepe
Over mine eies, to banish carelesse sleepe.

Yet oft my trembling eyes through faintnes close,
And then the Mappe of hell before me stands,
Which Ghosts doe see, and I am one of those
Ordain'd to pine in sorrowes endles bands,
Since from my wretched soule all hopes are reft
And now no cause of life to me is left.

Griefe ceaze my soule, for that will still endure
When my cras'd bodie is consum'd and gone,
Bear it to thy blacke denne, there keepe it sure,
Where thou ten thousand soules doest tyre upon.
Yet all doe not affoord such foode to thee
As this poore one, the worser part of mee.

X

Follow your Saint, follow with accents sweet,
Haste you, sad noates, fall at her flying feete:
There, wrapt in cloud of sorrowe pitie move,
And tell the ravisher of my soule, I perish for her love.
But if she scorns my never-ceasing paine,
Then burst with sighing in her sight, and nere returne againe.

All that I soong still to her praise did tend,
Still she was first, still she my songs did end.
Yet she my love, and Musicke both doeth flie,
The Musicke that her Eccho is, and beauties simpathie;
Then let my Noates pursue her scornefull flight:
It shall suffice, that they were breath'd, and dyed, for her delight.

XII

Thou art not faire for all thy red and white,
For all those rosie ornaments in thee,
Thou art not sweet though made of meer delight,
Nor faire nor sweet unlesse thou pitie mee.
I will not sooth thy fancies: thou shalt prove
That beauty is no beautie without love.

Yet love not me, nor seeke thou to allure
My thoughts with beautie, were it more devine;
Thy smiles and kisses I cannot endure,
I'le not be wrapt up in those armes of thine.
Now shew it, if thou be a woman right,
Embrace, and kisse, and love me in despight.

XIII

See where she flies enrag'd from me,
View her when she intends despite,
The winde is not more swift than shee,
Her furie mov'd such terror makes,
As to a fearfull guiltie sprite
The voice of heav'ns huge thunder cracks:
But when her appeased minde yeelds to delight,
All her thoughts are made of joies,
Millions of delights inventing:
Other pleasures are but toies
To her beauties sweete contenting.

My fortune hangs upon her brow,
For as she smiles or frownes on mee,
So must my blowne affections bow;
And her proude thoughts too well do find
With what unequal tyrannie
Her beauties doe command my mind.

Though, when her sad planet raignes, froward she bee,
She alone can pleasure move,
And displeasing sorrow banish.
May I but still hold her love,
Let all other comforts vanish.

XIV

Blame not my cheeks, though pale with love they be;
The kindly heate unto my heart is flowne,
To cherish it that is dismaid by thee,
Who art so cruell and unsteedfast growne:
For nature, cald for by distressed harts,
Neglects and quite forsakes the outward partes.

But they whose cheekes with careles blood are stain'd
Nurse not one sparke of love within their harts,
And when they woe they speake with passion fain'd,
For their fat love lyes in their outward parts:
But in their brests where love his court should hold,
Poore Cupid sits, and blowes his nailes for cold.

XX

When thou must home to shades of under ground,
And there ariv'd, a newe admired guest,
The beauteous spirits do ingirt thee round,
White Iope, blith Hellen, and the rest,
To heare the stories of thy finisht love,
From that smoothe toong whose musicke hell can move;

Then wilt thou speake of banqueting delights,
Of masks and revels which sweete youth did make,
Of Turnies and great challenges of knights,
And all these triumphes for thy beauties sake:
When thou hast told these honours done to thee,
Then tell, O tell, how thou didst murther me.

XXI

Come, let us sound with melody the praises
Of the kings king, th' omnipotent creator,
Author of number, that hath all the world in
                Harmonie framed.

Heav'n is His throne perpetually shining,
His devine power and glorie thence he thunders,
One in all, and all still in one abiding,
              Both Father, and Sonne.

O sacred sprite, invisible, eternall,
Ev'ry where, yet unlimited, that all things
Canst in one moment penetrate, revive me,
              O holy Spirit.

Rescue, O rescue me from earthly darknes,
Banish hence all these elementall objects,
Guide my soule, that thirsts, to the lively Fountaine
              Of thy devinenes.

Cleanse my soule, O God, thy bespotted Image,
Altered with sinne, so that heav'nly purenes
Cannot acknowledge me but in thy mercies,
              O Father of grace.

But when once thy beames do remove my darknes,
O then I'le shine forth as an Angell of light,
And record with more than an earthly voice thy
              Infinite honours.

From *Two Bookes of Ayres* (1613?)

1. Divine and Morall Songs

To the Reader

Out of many Songs which partly at the request of friends, partly for my owne recreation were by mee long since composed, I have now enfranchised a few, sending them forth divided according to their different subject into severall Bookes. The first are grave and pious; the second amorous and light. For hee that in publishing any worke, hath a desire to content all palates, must cater for them accordingly.

— Non omnibus unum est
Quod placet, hic Spinas colligit, ille Rosas.

[No one thing pleases all: one picks thorns, another roses.]

These Ayres were for the most part framed at first for one voyce with the Lute, or Violl, but upon occasion, they have since beene filled with more parts, which who so please may use, who like not may leave. Yet doe wee daily observe, that when any shall sing a Treble to an Instrument, the standers by will be offring at an inward part out of their owne nature; and true or false, out it must, though to the perverting of the whole harmonie. Also, if wee consider well, the Treble tunes, which are with us commonly called Ayres, are but Tenors mounted eight Notes higher, and therefore an inward part must needes well become them, such as may take up the whole distance of the Diapason [the octave] *, and fill up the gaping betweene the two extreame parts; whereby though they are not three parts in perfection, yet they yeeld a sweetnesse and content both to the eare and minde, which is the ayme and perfection of Musicke. Short Ayres if they be skilfully framed, and naturally exprest, are like quicke and good Epigrammes in Poesie, many of them shewing as much artifice, and breeding as great difficultie as a larger Poeme.* Non omnia possumus omnes, *said the* Romane *Epick Poet.* [Virgil, *Eclogues*, VIII: 'We cannot all do all things.'] *But some there are who admit onely* French *or* Italian *Ayres, as if every Country had not his proper Ayre, which the people thereof naturally usurpe in their Musicke. Others taste nothing that comes forth in Print, as if* Catullus *or* Martials *Epigrammes were the worse for being published. In these* English *Ayres I have chiefely* *aymed to couple my Words and Notes lovingly together, which will be much for him to doe that hath not power over both. The light of this will best appeare to him who hath pays'd* [weighed] *our Monasyllables and Syllables combined, both which are so loaded with Consonants as that they will hardly keepe company with swift Notes, or give the Vowell convenient liberty. To conclude; mine owne opinion of these Songs I deliver thus:*

>   Omnia nec nostris bona sunt, sed nec mala libris;
>   Si placet hac cantes, hac quoque lege legas.

['Not all the things in our book are good, nor are all of them bad; you may sing them if you like, or read them, on this understanding.' Martial I. xvi.]

I

>   Author of light, revive my dying spright,
>   Redeeme it from the snares of all-confounding night.
>   Lord, light me to thy blessed way:
>   For blinde with worldly vaine desires, I wander as a stray.
>   Sunne and Moone, Starres and underlights I see,
>   But all their glorious beames are mists and darknes being compar'd to thee.

>   Fountaine of health, my soules deepe wounds recure,
>   Sweet showres of pitty raine, wash my uncleannesse pure.
>   One drop of thy desired grace
>   The faint and fading hart can raise, and in joyes bosome place.
>   Sinne and Death, Hell and tempting Fiends may rage;
>   But God his owne will guard, and their sharp paines and griefe in time asswage.

II

>   The man of life upright,
>   Whose chearfull minde is free
>   From waight of impious deedes
>   And yoake of vanitee;

>   The man whose silent dayes
>   In harmlesse joyes are spent:
>   Whom hopes cannot delude,
>   Nor sorrowes discontent;

That man needes neyther towres,
   Nor armour for defence:
Nor vaults his guilt to shrowd
   From thunders violence;

Hee onely can behold
   With unaffrighted eyes
The horrors of the deepe,
   And terrors of the Skies.

Thus, scorning all the cares
   That fate or fortune brings,
His Booke the Heav'ns hee makes,
   His wisedome heav'nly things;

Good thoughts his surest friends,
   His wealth a well-spent age,
The earth his sober Inne,
   And quiet pilgrimage.

III

Where are all thy beauties now all harts enchayning?
Whither are thy flatt'rers gone with all their fayning?
All fled, and thou alone still here remayning.

Thy rich state of twisted gold to Bayes is turned;
Cold as thou art, are thy loves that so much burned:
Who dye in flatt'rers armes are seldome mourned.

Yet in spight of envie, this be still proclaymed,
That none worthyer than thy selfe thy worth hath blamed:
When their poore names are lost, thou shalt live famed.

When thy story long time hence shall be perused,
Let the blemish of thy rule be thus excused:
None ever liv'd more just, none more abused.

V

View mee, Lord, a worke of thine:
Shall I then lye drown'd in night?
Might thy grace in mee but shine,
I should seeme made all of light.

But my soule still surfets so
On the poysoned baytes of sinne,
That I strange and ugly growe,
All in darke, and foule within.

Clense mee, Lord, that I may kneele
At thine Altar, pure and white:
They that once thy Mercies feele,
Gaze no more on earths delight.

Worldly joyes like shadowes fade,
When the heav'nly light appeares;
But the cov'nants thou hast made,
Endlesse, know nor dayes, nor yeares.

In thy word, Lord, is my trust,
To thy mercies fast I flye;
Though I am but clay and dust,
Yet thy grace can lift me high.

VII

To Musicke bent is my retyred minde,
And faine would I some song of pleasure sing:
But in vaine joyes no comfort now I finde:
From heav'nly thoughts all true delight doth spring.
Thy power, O God, thy mercies to record
Will sweeten ev'ry note and ev'ry word.

All earthly pompe or beauty to expresse,
Is but to carve in snow, on waves to write.
Celestiall things, though men conceive them lesse,
Yet fullest are they in themselves of light:
Such beames they yeeld as know no meanes to dye:
Such heate they cast as lifts the Spirit high.

VIII

Tune thy Musicke to thy hart,
Sing thy joy with thankes, and so thy sorrow:
Though Devotion needes not Art,
Sometime of the poore the rich may borrow.

    Strive not yet for curious wayes:
Concord pleaseth more, the lesse 'tis strained;
    Zeale affects not outward prayse,
Onely strives to shew a love unfained.

    Love can wondrous things effect,
Sweetest Sacrifice, all wrath appeasing:
    Love the highest doth respect,
Love alone to him is ever pleasing.

IX

    Most sweet and pleasing are thy wayes, O God,
Like Meadowes deckt with Christall streames and flowers:
Thy paths no foote prophane hath ever trod:
Nor hath the proud man rested in thy Bowers.
    There lives no Vultur, no devouring Beare,
But onely Doves and Lambs are harbor'd there.

The Wolfe his young ones to their prey doth guide;
The Foxe his Cubbs with false deceit endues;
The Lyons Whelpe suckes from his Damme his pride;
In hers the Serpent malice doth infuse:
    The darksome Desart all such beasts contaynes,
Not one of them in Paradice remaynes.

X

    Wise men patience never want,
Good men pitty cannot hide:
Feeble spirits onely vant
Of revenge, the poorest pride.
Hee alone, forgive that can,
Beares the true soule of a man.

Some there are, debate that seeke,
Making trouble their content,
Happy if they wrong the meeke,
Vexe them that to peace are bent:
Such undooe the common tye
Of mankinde, societie.

Kindnesse growne is, lately, colde,
Conscience hath forgot her part:

Blessed times were knowne of old,
Long ere Law became an Art.
Shame deterr'd, not Statutes then,
Honest love was law to men.

Deeds from love, and words, that flowe
Foster like kinde *Aprill* showres;
In the warme Sunne all things grow,
Wholsome fruits and pleasant flowres.
All so thrives his gentle rayes,
Where on humane love displayes.

XI

Never weather-beaten Saile more willing bent to shore,
Never tyred Pilgrims limbs affected slumber more,
Than my wearied spright now longs to flye out of my troubled
                                                       brest.
  O come quickly, sweetest Lord, and take my soule to rest.

Ever-blooming are the joyes of Heav'ns high paradice,
Cold age deafes not there our eares, nor vapour dims our eyes;
Glory there the Sun outshines, whose beames the blessed onely see;
  O come quickly, glorious Lord, and raise my spright to thee.

XIII

Loe, when backe mine eye,
    Pilgrim-like, I cast,
What fearefull wayes I spye,
Which blinded I securely past!

But now heav'n hath drawne
    From my browes that night;
As when the day doth dawne,
So cleares my long imprison'd sight.

Straight the caves of hell
    Drest with flowres I see,
Wherein false pleasures dwell,
That, winning most, most deadly be.

Throngs of masked Feinds
    Wing'd like Angels flye,

Even in the gates of Friends;
In faire disguise blacke dangers lye.

Straight to Heav'n I rais'd
  My restored sight,
And with loud voyce I prais'd
The Lord of ever-during light.

And, since I had stray'd
  From his wayes so wide,
His grace I, humble, pray'd
Hence-forth to be my guard and guide.

XVI

Awake, awake thou heavy spright,
That sleep'st the deadly sleepe of sinne;
  Rise now and walke the waies of light:
'Tis not too late yet to begin.
    Seeke heaven earely, seeke it late;
    True faith still findes an open gate.

Get up, get up thou leaden man:
Thy tracks to endlesse joy, or paine,
  Yeelds but the modell of a span;
Yet burnes out thy lifes lampe in vaine.
    One minute bounds thy bane, or blisse,
    Then watch, and labour while time is.

XVII

Come, chearfull day, part of my life, to mee:
For while thou view'st me with thy fading light,
Part of my life doth still depart with thee,
And I still onward haste to my last night.
  Times fatall wings doe ever forward flye,
  Soe ev'ry day we live, a day wee dye.

But O yee nights ordain'd for barren rest,
How are my dayes depriv'd of life in you,
When heavy sleepe my soule hath dispossest,
By fayned death life sweetly to renew!
  Part of my life in that, you life denye:
  So ev'ry day we live, a day wee dye.

XVIII

Seeke the Lord, and in his wayes persever!
O faint not, but as Eagles flye,
For his steepe hill is high;
Then striving gaine the top, and triumph ever.

When with glory there thy browes are crowned,
New joys so shall abound in thee,
Such sights thy soule shall see,
That worldly thoughts shall by their beames be drowned.

Farewell World, thou masse of meere confusion,
False light with many shadowes dimm'd,
Old Witch with new foyles trimm'd,
Thou deadly sleepe of soule, and charm'd illusion.

I the King will seek, of Kings adored,
Spring of light, tree of grace and blisse,
Whose fruit so sov'raigne is,
That all who taste it are from death restored.

XXI

All lookes be pale, harts cold as stone,
For *Hally* now is dead, and gone,
Hally, in whose sight,
Most sweet sight,
All the earth late tooke delight.
Ev'ry eye weepe with mee,
Joyes drown'd in teares must be.

His Iv'ry skin, his comely hayre,
His Rosie cheekes so cleare and faire:
Eyes that once did grace
His bright face,
Now in him all want their place.
Eyes and hearts weepe with mee,
For who so kinde as hee?

His youth was like an *Aprill* flowre,
Adorn'd with beauty, love, and powre,
Glory strow'd his way,

> Whose wreaths gay
> Now are all turn'd to decay.
Then againe weepe with mee,
None feele more cause than wee.

No more may his wisht sight returne,
His golden Lampe no more can burne;
> Quencht is all his flame,
> His hop't fame
> Now hath left him nought but name.
For him all weepe with mee
Since more him none shall see.

2. Light Conceits of Lovers

To the Reader

That holy Hymnes with Lovers cares are knit
Both in one Quire here, thou maist think't unfit.
Why do'st not blame the Stationer as well,
Who in the same Shop sets all sorts to sell?
Divine with stiles prophane, grave shelv'd with vaine,
And some matcht worse; yet none of him complaine.

I

Vaine men whose follies make a God of Love,
Whose blindnesse beauty doth immortall deeme,
Prayse not what you desire, but what you prove,
Count those things good that are, not those that seeme.
I cannot call her true that's false to me,
Nor make of women more than women be.

How faire an entrance breakes the way to love!
How rich of golden hope, and gay delight!
What hart cannot a modest beauty move?
Who seeing cleare day once will dreame of night?
Shee seem'd a Saint, that brake her faith with mee,
But prov'd a woman as all other be.

So bitter is their sweet, that true content
Unhappy men in them may never finde;

Ah, but without them, none; both must consent,
Else uncouth are the joyes of eyther kinde.
Let us then prayse their good, forget their ill:
Men must be men, and women women still.

III

Harden now thy tyred hart, with more than flinty rage;
Ne'er let her false teares henceforth thy constant griefe asswage.
Once true happy dayes thou saw'st, when shee stood firme and
                                        kinde:
Both as one then liv'd, and held one eare, one tongue, one minde.
But now those bright houres be fled, and never may returne:
What then remaines, but her untruths to mourne?

Silly Traytresse, who shall now thy careless tresses place?
Who thy pretty talke supply? whose eare thy musicke grace?
Who shall thy bright eyes admire? what lips triumph with thine?
Day by day who'll visit thee and say 'th'art onely mine'?
Such a time there was, God wot, but such shall never be:
Too oft I feare thou wilt remember me.

IV

O what unhop't for sweet supply!
   O what joyes exceeding!
What an affecting charme feele I,
   From delight proceeding!
That which I long despair'd to be,
   To her I am, and shee to mee.

Shee that alone in cloudy griefe
   Long to mee appeared,
Shee now alone with bright reliefe
   All those clouds hath cleared.
Both are immortall, and divine,
   Since I am hers, and she is mine.

VII

    Give beauty all her right,
    Shee's not to one forme tyed;
    Each shape yeelds faire delight
    Where her perfections bide.

Hellen I grant might pleasing be;
And *Ros'mond* was as sweet as shee.

    Some the quicke eye commends,
    Some swelling lips and red;
    Pale lookes have many friends,
    Through sacred sweetnesse bred.
Medowes have flowres that pleasure move,
Though Roses are the flowres of love.

    Free beauty is not bound
    To one unmoved clime,
    She visits ev'ry ground,
    And favours ev'ry time.
Let the old loves with mine compare,
My sov'raigne is as sweet, and fayre.

IX

Good men, shew, if you can tell,
Where doth humane pittie dwell?
Farre and neere her would I seeke,
So vext with sorrow is my brest.
She (they say) to all is meeke,
And onely makes th' unhappie blest.

Oh! if such a Saint there be,
Some hope yet remaines for me:
Prayer or sacrifice may gaine
From her implored grace reliefe,
To release mee of my paine,
Or at the least to ease my griefe.

Young am I, and farre from guile,
The more is my woe the while:
Falshood with a smooth disguise
My simple meaning hath abus'd,
Casting mists before mine eyes,
By which my senses are confus'd.

Fair he is, who vow'd to me
That he onely mine would be:

But alas, his minde is caught
With ev'ry gaudie bait he sees.
And too late my flame is taught
That too much kindnesse makes men freese.

From me all my friends are gone,
While I pine for him alone,
And not one will rue my case,
But rather my distresse deride:
That I thinke there is no place
Where pittie ever yet did bide.

X

What harvest halfe so sweet is
As still to reape the kisses
   Growne ripe in sowing?
And straight to be receiver
Of that which thou art giver,
   Rich in bestowing?
Kisse then, my harvest Queene,
   Full garners heaping;
Kisses, ripest when th'are greene,
   Want onely reaping.

The Dove alone expresses
Her fervencie in kisses,
   Of all most loving:
A creature as offencelesse
As those things that are sencelesse
   And void of moving.
Let us so love and kisse,
   Though all envy us:
That which kinde, and harmlesse is,
   None can denie us.

XI

Sweet, exclude mee not, nor be divided
   From him that ere long must bed thee:
All thy maiden doubts Law hath decided;
   Sure wee are, and I must wed thee.
   Presume then yet a little more:
     Here's the way, barre not the dore.

Tenants, to fulfill their Land-lords pleasure,
 Pay their rent before the quarter:
'Tis my case, if you it rightly measure;
 Put mee not then off with laughter.
Consider then a little more:
 Here's the way to all my store.

Why were dores in loves despight devised?
 Are not Lawes enough restrayning?
Women are most apt to be surprised
 Sleeping, or sleepe wisely fayning.
Then grace me yet a little more:
 Here's the way, barre not the dore.

XII

 The peacefull westerne winde
 The winter stormes hath tam'd,
 And nature in each kinde
 The kinde heat hath inflam'd.
The forward buds so sweetly breathe
 Out of their earthy bowers,
That heav'n which viewes their pompe beneath
 Would faine be deckt with flowers.

 See how the morning smiles
 On her bright easterne hill,
 And with soft steps beguiles
 Them that lie slumbring still.
The musicke-loving birds are come
 From cliffes and rockes unknowne,
To see the trees and briers blome,
 That late were overflowne.

 What Saturne did destroy,
 Loves Queene revives againe;
 And now her naked boy
 Doth in the fields remaine:
Where he such pleasing change doth view
 In ev'ry living thing,
As if the world were borne anew
 To gratifie the Spring.

If all things life present,
Why die my comforts then?
Why suffers my content?
Am I the worst of men?
O beautie, be not thou accus'd
 Too justly in this case:
Unkindly if true love be us'd,
 'Twill yeeld thee little grace.

XIII

There is none, O none but you,
 That from mee estrange your sight,
Whom mine eyes affect to view,
 Or chained eares heare with delight.

Other beauties others move,
 In you I all graces finde:
Such is the effect of love,
 To make them happy that are kinde.

Women in fraile beauty trust,
 Onely seeme you faire to mee;
Yet prove truely kinde and just,
 For that may not dissembled be.

Sweet, afford mee then your sight,
 That, survaying all your lookes,
Endlesse volumes I may write,
 And fill the world with envyed bookes:

Which when after ages view,
 All shall wonder, and despaire,
Woman to finde man so true,
 Or man a woman halfe so faire.

XIV

Pin'd I am, and like to die,
And all for lacke of that which I
 Doe ev'ry day refuse.
If I musing sit, or stand,
Some puts it daily in my hand,
 To interrupt my muse.

The same thing I seeke, and flie,
And want that which none would denie.

In my bed, when I should rest,
It breeds such trouble in my brest
   That scarce mine eyes will close:
If I sleepe, it seemes to be
Oft playing in the bed with me,
   But, wak't, away it goes.
'Tis some spirit sure, I weene,
And yet it may be felt, and seene.

Would I had the heart, and wit
To make it stand, and conjure it
   That haunts me thus with feare.
Doubtlesse tis some harmlesse spright,
For it by day, as well as night,
   Is ready to appeare.
Be it friend, or be it foe,
Ere long Ile trie what it will doe.

XVI

Though your strangenesse frets my hart,
Yet may not I complaine:
You perswade me, 'tis but Art,
That secret love must faine.
If another you affect,
'Tis but a shew t'avoid suspect.
Is this faire excusing? O no, all is abusing.

Your wisht sight if I desire,
Suspitions you pretend,
Causelesse you your selfe retire,
While I in vaine attend:
This a Lover whets, you say,
Still made more eager by delay.
Is this faire excusing? O no, all is abusing.

When another holds your hand,
You sweare I hold your hart:
When my Rivals close doe stand

And I sit farre apart,
I am neerer yet than they,
Hid in your bosome, as you say.
Is this faire excusing? O no, all is abusing.

Would my Rival then I were,
Some els your secret friend:
So much lesser should I feare,
And not so much attend.
They enjoy you, ev'ry one,
Yet I must seeme your friend alone.
Is this faire excusing? O no, all is abusing.

XVII

Come away, arm'd with loves delights,
  Thy sprightfull graces bring with thee:
 When love with longing fights
  They must the sticklers be.
Come quickly, come, the promis'd houre is wel-nye spent,
And pleasure being too much deferr'd looseth her best content.

Is shee come? O, how neare is shee?
  How farre yet from this friendly place?
 How many steps from me?
  When shall I her imbrace?
These armes Ile spred which onely at her sight shall close,
Attending as the starry flowre, that the Suns noone-tide knowes.

XVIII

Come, you pretty false-ey'd wanton,
  Leave your crafty smiling:
Thinke you to escape me now
  With slipp'ry words beguiling?
No; you mock't me th'other day,
  When you got loose, you fled away;
But since I have caught you now,
  Ile clip your wings for flying:
Smothring kisses fast Ile heape,
  And keepe you so from crying.

Sooner may you count the starres,
  And number hayle downe pouring,

49

Tell the Osiers of the *Temmes*,
    Or *Goodwins* Sands devouring,
Than the thicke-showr'd kisses here
    Which now thy tyred lips must beare;
Such a harvest never was,
    So rich and full of pleasure,
But 'tis spent as soone as reapt,
    So trustlesse is loves treasure.

Would it were dumb midnight now,
    When all the world lyes sleeping:
Would this place some Desert were,
    Which no man hath in keeping.
My desires should then be safe,
    And when you cry'd then would I laugh;
But if ought might breed offence,
    Love onely should be blamed:
I would live your servant still,
    And you my Saint unnamed.

XIX

A secret love or two, I must confesse,
    I kindly welcome for change in close playing:
Yet my deare husband I love ne'erthelesse,
    His desires, whole or halfe, quickly allaying,
At all times ready to offer redresse.
    His owne he never wants, but hath it duely,
    Yet twits me I keepe not touch with him truly.

The more a spring is drawne, the more it flowes;
    No Lampe lesse light retaines by lightning others:
Is hee a looser his losse that ne're knowes?
    Or is he wealthy that wast treasure smothers?
My churle vowes no man shall sent his sweet Rose,
    His owne enough and more I give him duely,
    Yet still he twits mee I keepe not touch truly.

Wise Archers beare more than one shaft to field,
    The Venturer loads not with one ware his shipping:
Should Warriers learn but one weapon to weilde?
    Or thrive faire plants ere the worse for the slipping?

One dish cloyes, many fresh appetite yeeld:
    Mine own Ile use, and his he shall have duely,
    Judge then what debter can keepe touch more truly.

From the *Third Booke of Ayres* (1617?)

To my Honourable Friend, Sir Thomas Mounson, *Knight and Baronet*

Since now those clouds, that lately over-cast
Your Fame and Fortune, are disperst at last:
And now since all to you fayre greetings make,
Some out of love, and some for pitties sake:
Shall I but with a common stile salute
Your new enlargement? or stand onely mute?
I, to whose trust and care you durst commit
Your pined health, when Arte despayr'd of it?
I, that in your afflicition often view'd
In you the fruits of manly fortitude,
Patience, and even constancie of minde,
That Rocke-like stood, and scorn'd both wave, and winde?
Should I, for all your ancient love to me,
Endow'd with waighty favours, silent be?
Your merits and my gratitude forbid
That eyther should in Lethean *Gulfe lye hid.*
But how shall I this worke of fame expresse?
How can I better, after pensivenesse,
Than with light straynes of Musicke, made to move
Sweetly with the wide-spreading plumes of love?
These youth-borne Ayres, *then, prison'd in this Booke,*
Which in your Bowres much of their beeing tooke,
Accept as a kinde offring from that hand
Which joyn'd with heart, your vertue may command.
Who love a sure friend, as all good men doe,
Since such you are, let those affect you to:
And may the joyes of that Crowne never end,
That innocence doth pitty, and defend.
                              Your devoted,
                                 Thomas Campian.

I

Oft have I sigh'd for him that heares me not:
Who absent hath both love and mee forgot.
Oh yet I languish still through his delay.
Dayes seeme as yeares when wisht friends breake their day.

Had hee but lov'd as common lovers use,
His faithlesse stay some kindnesse would excuse:
O yet I languish still, still constant mourne
For him that can breake vowes, but not returne.

III

Were my hart as some mens are, thy errours would not move me:
But thy faults I curious finde and speake because I love thee:
Patience is a thing divine, and farre, I grant, above me.

Foes sometimes befriend us more, our blacker deedes objecting,
Than th'obsequious bosome guest, with false respect affecting:
Friendship is the glasse of Truth, our hidden staines detecting.

While I use of eyes enjoy, and inward light of reason,
Thy observer will I be, and censor, but in season:
Hidden mischiefe to conceale in State and Love is treason.

IV

Maydes are simple, some men say,
They, forsooth, will trust no men:
But should they mens wils obey,
Maides were very simple then.

Truth a rare flower now is growne,
Few men weare it in their hearts;
Lovers are more easily knowne
By their follies, than deserts.

Safer may we credit give
To a faithlesse wandring Jew,
Than a young mans vowes beleeve,
When he sweares his love is true.

Love they make a poore blinde childe,
But let none trust such as hee;
Rather than to be beguil'd,
Ever let me simple be.

V

So tyr'd are all my thoughts, that sence and spirits faile;
Mourning I pine, and know not what I ayle.

O what can yeeld ease to a minde,
        Joy in nothing that can finde?

How are my powres fore-spoke? What strange distaste is this?
Hence, cruell hate of that which sweetest is:
Come, come delight, make my dull braine
        Feele once heate of joy againe.

The lovers teares are sweet, their mover makes them so:
Proud of a wound the bleeding Souldiers grow:
Poore I alone, dreaming, endure
        Grief that knowes nor cause, nor cure.

And whence can all this grow? even from an idle minde,
That no delight in any good can finde.
Action alone makes the soule blest;
        Vertue dyes with too much rest.

VII

    Kinde are her answeres,
        But her performance keeps no day,
    Breaks time, as dancers
        From their own Musicke when they stray:
        All her free favors
And smooth words wing my hopes in vaine.
O did ever voice so sweet but only fain?
        Can true love yeeld such delay,
        Converting joy to pain?

    Lost is our freedome,
        When we submit to women so:
Why doe wee neede them,
        When in their best they worke our woe?
        There is no wisdome
Can alter ends by Fate prefixt;
O why is the good of man with evill mixt?
        Never were days yet cal'd two,
        But one night went betwixt.

VIII

O griefe, O spight, to see poore Vertue scorn'd,
Truth far exil'd, False arte lov'd, Vice ador'd,
Free Justice sold, worst causes best adorn'd,
Right cast by Powre, Pittie in vaine implor'd!
  O who in such an age could wish to live,
  When none can have or hold, but such as give?

O times! O men! to Nature rebels growne;
Poore in desert; in name rich; proud of shame;
Wise but in ill: your stiles are not your owne,
Though dearely bought, honour is honest fame.
  Old Stories onely goodnesse now containe,
  And the true wisedome, that is just, and plaine.

X

Breake now my heart and dye! Oh no, she may relent.
Let my despaire prevayle! Oh stay, hope is not spent.
Should she now fixe one smile on thee, where were despaire?
  The losse is but easie which smiles can repayre.
  A stranger would please thee, if she were as fayre.

Her must I love or none, so sweet none breathes as shee;
The more is my despayre, alas shee loves not mee:
But cannot time make way for love through ribs of steele?
  The Grecian, inchanted all parts but the heele,
  At last a shaft daunted, which his hart did feele.

XI

If Love loves truth, then women doe not love;
Their passions all are but dissembled shewes;
Now kinde and free of favour if they prove,
Their kindnes straight a tempest overthrowes.
  Then as a Sea-man the poore lover fares,
  The storme drownes him ere hee can drowne his cares.

But why accuse I women that deceive?
Blame then the Foxes for their subtile wile:
They first from Nature did their craft receive:
It is a womans nature to beguile.
  Yet some, I grant, in loving stedfast grow;
  But such by use are made, not nature, so.

O why had Nature power at once to frame
Deceit and Beauty, traitors both to Love?
O would Deceit had dyed when Beauty came
With her divinenesse ev'ry heart to move!
    Yet doe we rather wish, what ere befall,
    To have fayre women false, than none at all.

XII

Now winter nights enlarge
    The number of their houres,
And clouds their stormes discharge
    Upon the ayrie towres:
Let now the chimneys blaze,
    And cups o'erflow with wine:
Let well-tun'd words amaze
    With harmonie divine.
Now yellow waxen lights
    Shall waite on hunny Love,
While youthfull Revels, Masks, and Courtly sights,
    Sleepes leaden spels remove.

This time doth well dispence
    With lovers long discourse;
Much speech hath some defence,
    Though beauty no remorse.
All doe not all things well;
    Some measures comely tread,
Some knotted Ridles tell,
    Some Poems smoothly read.
The Summer hath his joyes,
    And Winter his delights;
Though Love and all his pleasures are but toyes,
    They shorten tedious nights.

XV

Fire that must flame is with apt fuell fed,
Flowers that wil thrive in sunny soyle are bred;
How can a hart feele heate that no hope findes?
Or can hee love on whom no comfort shines?

Fayre, I confesse there's pleasure in your sight:
Sweet, you have powre, I grant, of all delight:

But what is all to mee, if I have none?
Churle that you are, t'injoy such wealth alone.

Prayers move the heav'ns, but finde no grace with you;
Yet in your lookes a heavenly forme I view:
Then will I pray againe, hoping to finde
As well as in your lookes, heav'n in your minde.

Saint of my heart, Queene of my life, and love,
O let my vowes thy loving spirit move:
Let me no longer mourne through thy disdaine,
But with one touch of grace cure all my paine.

XVI
If thou long'st so much to learne (sweet boy) what 'tis to love,
Doe but fixe thy thought on mee, and thou shalt quickly prove.
    Little sute, at first, shal win
        Way to thy abasht desire:
    But then will I hedge thee in,
        Salamander-like with fire.

With thee dance I will, and sing, and thy fond dalliance beare;
Wee the grovy hils will climbe, and play the wantons there;
    Other whiles wee'le gather flowres,
        Lying dalying on the grasse,
    And thus our delightfull howres
        Full of waking dreames shall passe.

When thy joyes were thus at height, my love should turne from thee,
Old acquaintance then should grow as strange as strange might be;
    Twenty rivals thou should'st finde
        Breaking all their hearts for mee,
    When to all Ile prove more kinde,
        And more forward than to thee.

Thus thy silly youth, enrag'd, would soone my love defie;
But, alas poore soule, too late; clipt wings can never flye:
    Those sweet houres which wee had past
        Cal'd to minde, thy heart would burne:
    And could'st thou flye ne'er so fast,
        They would make thee straight returne.

XVII

Shall I come, sweet Love, to thee,
  When the ev'ning beames are set?
Shall I not excluded be?
  Will you finde no fained lett?
    Let me not, for pitty, more,
    Tell the long houres at your dore.

Who can tell what theefe or foe,
  In the covert of the night,
For his prey, will worke my woe,
  Or through wicked foule despight:
    So may I dye unredrest,
    Ere my long love be possest.

But to let such dangers passe,
  Which a lovers thoughts disdaine,
'Tis enough in such a place
  To attend loves joyes in vaine.
    Doe not mocke me in thy bed,
    While these cold nights freeze me dead.

XVIII

Thrice tosse these Oaken ashes in the ayre;
Thrice sit thou mute in this inchanted chayre:
Then thrice three times tye up this true loves knot,
And murmur soft shee will, or shee will not.

Goe burne these poys'nous weedes in yon blew fire,
These Screech-owles fethers, and this prickling bryer,
This Cypresse gathered at a dead mans grave;
That all thy feares and cares an end may have.

Then come, you Fayries, dance with me a round,
Melt her hard hart with your melodious sound.
In vaine are all the charms I can devise:
She hath an Arte to breake them with her eyes.

XX

  Fire, fire, fire, fire!
Loe here I burne in such desire
That all the teares that I can straine

Out of mine idle empty braine
Cannot allay my scorching paine.
    Come *Trent*, and *Humber*, and fayre *Thames*,
    Dread Ocean haste with all thy streames;
    And if you cannot quench my fire,
    O drowne both mee and my desire.

    Fire, fire, fire, fire!
There is no hell to my desire:
See all the Rivers backward flye,
And th' Ocean doth his waves deny,
For feare my heate should drinke them dry.
    Come, heav'nly showres, then, pouring downe;
    Come you that once the world did drowne:
    Some then you spar'd, but now save all,
    That else must burne, and with mee fall.

XXI

O sweet delight, O more than humane blisse,
With her to live that ever loving is:
To heare her speake, whose words so well are plac't,
That she by them, as they in her are grac't:
    Those lookes to view that feast the viewers eye;
    How blest is he that may so live and dye!

Such love as this the golden times did know,
When all did reape, yet none tooke care to sow:
Such love as this an endlesse Summer makes,
And all distaste from fraile affection takes.
    So lov'd, so blest, in my belov'd am I;
    Which till their eyes ake let yron men envy.

XXII

Thus I resolve, and time hath taught me so:
Since she is fayre and ever kinde to me,
Though she be wilde and wanton-like in shew,
Those little staines in youth I will not see:
    That she be constant, heaven I oft implore;
    If pray'rs prevaile not, I can doe no more.

Palme tree the more you presse, the more it growes,
Leave it alone, it will not much exceede.

Free beauty if you strive to yoke, you lose,
And for affection strange distaste you breede.
    What Nature hath not taught no Arte can frame;
    Wilde borne be wilde still, though by force made tame.

XXIII

Come, O come my lifes delight,
Let me not in langour pine:
    Love loves no delay: thy sight,
The more enjoy'd, the more divine.
        O come and take from mee
        The paine of being depriv'd of thee.

Thou all sweetnesse dost enclose,
Like a little world of blisse:
    Beauty guards thy lookes, the Rose
In them pure and eternall is.
        Come then, and make thy flight
        As swift to me as heav'nly light.

XXV

Sleepe, angry beauty, sleep, and feare not me;
For who a sleeping Lyon dares provoke?
It shall suffice me here to sit and see
Those lips shut up that never kindely spoke.
    What sight can more content a lovers minde
    Than beauty seeming harmlesse, if not kinde?

My words have charm'd her, for secure shee sleepes,
Though guilty much of wrong done to my love;
And in her slumber, see, shee close-ey'd weepes;
Dreames often more than waking passions move.
    Pleade, sleepe, my cause, and make her soft like thee,
    That shee in peace may wake and pitty mee.

XXVI

Silly boy, 'tis ful Moone yet, thy night as day shines clearely;
Had thy youth but wit to feare, thou couldst not love so dearely.
Shortly wilt thou mourne when all thy pleasures are bereaved;
Little knowes he how to love that never was deceived.

This is thy first mayden flame that triumphes yet unstayned;
All is artlesse now you speake, not one word yet is fayned;
All is heav'n that you behold, and all your thoughts are blessed:
But no Spring can want his Fall, each *Troylus* hath his *Cresseid*.

Thy well-order'd lockes ere long shall rudely hang neglected;
And thy lively pleasant cheare, reade griefe on earth dejected.
Much then wilt thou blame thy Saint, that made thy heart so holy,
And with sighs confesse, in love, that too much faith is folly.

Yet be just and constant still; Love may beget a wonder,
Not unlike a Summers frost, or Winters fatall thunder:
He that holds his Sweet-hart true unto his day of dying
Lives of all that ever breath'd most worthy the envying.

XXVII

Never love unlesse you can
Beare with all the faults of man:
Men sometimes will jealous bee,
Though but little cause they see,
    And hang the head, as discontent,
    And speake what straight they will repent.

Men that but one Saint adore
Make a shew of love to more:
Beauty must be scorn'd in none,
Though but truely serv'd in one;
    For what is courtship, but disguise?
    True hearts may have dissembling eyes.

Men when their affaires require
Must a while themselves retire;
Sometimes hunt, and sometimes hawke,
And not ever sit and talke.
    If these and such like you can beare,
    Then like, and love, and never fear.

XXVIII

So quicke, so hot, so mad is thy fond sute,
So rude, so tedious growne in urging mee,
That faine I would with losse make thy tongue mute,

And yeeld some little grace to quiet thee.
    An houre with thee I care not to converse:
    For I would not be counted too perverse.

But roofes too hot would prove for men all fire,
And hils too high for my unused pace;
The grove is charg'd with thornes and the bold bryer;
Gray Snakes the meadowes shrowde in every place:
    A yellow Frog alas will fright me so
    As I should start and tremble as I goe.

Since then I can on earth no fit roome finde,
In heaven I am resolv'd with you to meete;
Till then for Hopes sweet sake rest your tir'd minde,
And not so much as see mee in the streete:
    A heavenly meeting one day wee shall have,
    But never, as you dreame, in bed, or grave.

From the *Fourth Booke of Ayres* (1617?)

To the Reader

The Apothecaries have Bookes of Gold, whose leaves being opened are so light as that they are subject to be shaken with the least breath, yet rightly handled, they serve both for ornament and use; such are light Ayres. But if any squeamish stomackes shall checke at two or three vaine Ditties in the end of this Booke, let them powre off the clearest, and leave those as dregs in the bottome. Howsoever, if they be but conferred with the Canterbury Tales *of that venerable Poet* Chaucer, *they will then appeare toothsome enough. Some words are in these Bookes, which have beene cloathed in Musicke by others, and I am content they then served their turne: yet give mee now leave to make use of mine owne. Likewise you may finde here some three or four Songs that have been published before, but for them, I referre you to the Players Bill that is stiled,* Newly revived with Additions, *for you shall finde all of them reformed eyther in Words or Notes. To be briefe, all these Songs are mine if you expresse them well, otherwise they are your owne. Farewell.*

Yours as you are his,
Thomas Campian.

II

Respect my faith, regard my service past;
The hope you wing'd call home to you at last.
Great prise it is that I in you shall gaine:
So great for you hath been my losse and paine.
    My wits I spent and time for you alone,
    Observing you and loosing all for one.

Some rais'd to rich estates in this time are,
That held their hopes to mine inferiour farre;
Such scoffing mee, or pittying me, say thus,
Had hee not lov'd he might have liv'd like us.
    O then deare sweet, for love and pitties sake,
    My faith reward, and from me scandall take.

IV

Vaile, love, mine eyes, O hide from me
The plagues that charge the curious minde:
If beauty private will not be,

Suffice it yet that she proves kinde.
Who can usurp heav'ns light alone?
Stars were not made to shine on one.

Griefes past recure fooles try to heale,
That greater harmes on lesse inflict:
The pure offend by too much zeale,
Affection should not be too strict.
    Hee that a true embrace will finde
    To beauties faults must still be blinde.

V

Ev'ry Dame affects good fame, what ere her doings be:
But true prayse is Vertues Bayes, which none may weare but she.
Borrow'd guise fits not the wise, a simple look is best:
Native grace becomes a face, though ne'er so rudely drest.
    Now such new found toyes are sold, these women to disguise,
    That before the yeare growes old the newest fashion dyes.

Dames of yore contended more in goodnesse to exceede,
Than in pride to be envi'd for that which least they neede:
Little Lawne then serv'd the Pawne, if Pawne at all there were;
Home-spun thread, and household bread then held out all the yeare.
    But th'attyres of women now weare out both house and land;
    That the wives in silkes may flow, at ebbe the Good-men stand.

Once agen *Astraea* then, from heav'n to earth descend,
And vouchsafe in their behalf these errours to amend:
Aid from heav'n must make all eev'n, things are so out of frame;
For let man strive all he can, hee needes must please his Dame.
    Happy man content that gives, and what hee gives, enjoyes;
    Happy Dame content that lives, and breakes no sleepe for toyes.

VII

There is a Garden in her face,
    Where Roses and white Lillies grow;
A heav'nly paradice is that place,
    Wherein all pleasant fruits doe flow.
    There Cherries grow which none may buy,
    Till Cherry ripe themselves doe cry.

Those Cherries fayrely doe enclose
Of Orient Pearle a double row,
  Which when her lovely laughter showes,
They look like Rose-buds fill'd with snow.
    Yet them nor Peere nor Prince can buy,
    Till Cherry ripe themselves doe cry.

Her Eyes like Angels watch them still;
Her Browes like bended bowes doe stand,
  Threatning with piercing frownes to kill
All that attempt with eye or hand
    Those sacred Cherries to come nigh,
    Till Cherry ripe themselves doe cry.

IX

Young and simple though I am,
I have heard of *Cupids* name:
Guesse I can what thing it is
Men desire when they doe kisse.
    Smoake can never burne, they say,
    But the flames that follow may.

I am not so foule or fayre,
To be proud, nor to despayre;
Yet my lips have oft observ'd,
Men that kisse them presse them hard,
    As glad lovers use to doe
    When their new met loves they wooe.

Faith, 'tis but a foolish minde,
Yet me thinkes a heate I finde,
Like thirst longing, that doth bide
Ever on my weaker side:
    Where they say my heart doth move.
    Venus grant it be not love.

If it be, alas, what then?
Were not women made for men?
As good 'twere a thing were past,
That must needes be done at last.
    Roses that are over-blowne
    Growe lesse sweet, then fall alone.

    Yet nor Churle, nor silken Gull
    Shall my Mayden blossome pull:
    Who shall not I soone can tell,
    Who shall, would I could as well:
       This I know, who ere hee be,
       Love hee must, or flatter me.

X

    Love me or not, love her I must or dye.
    Leave me or not, follow her needs must I.
    O that her grace would my wisht comforts give.
    How rich in her, how happy should I live!

    All my desire, all my delight should be
    Her to enjoy, her to unite to mee:
    Envy should cease, her would I love alone:
    Who loves by lookes, is seldome true to one.

    Could I enchant, and that it lawfull were,
    Her would I charme softly that none should heare.
    But love enforc'd rarely yeelds firme content;
    So would I love that neyther should repent.

XIII

    O Love, where are thy Shafts, thy Quiver and thy Bow?
    Shall my wounds onely weepe, and hee ungaged goe?
    Be just and strike him too, that dares contemne thee so.

    No eyes are like to thine, though men suppose thee blinde,
    So fayre they levell when the marke they list to finde:
    Then strike, o strike the heart that beares the cruell minde.

    Is my fond sight deceived? or doe I *Cupid* spye
    Close ayming at his breast, by whom despis'd I dye?
    Shoot home sweet *Love*, and wound him that hee may not flye!

    O then we both will sit in some unhaunted shade,
    And heale each others wound which *Love* hath justly made:
    O hope, o thought too vaine, how quickly dost thou fade!

    At large he wanders still, his heart is free from paine,
    While secret sighes I spend, and teares, but all in vaine:
    Yet *Love*, thou know'st, by right I should not thus complaine.

XIV

Beauty is but a painted hell,
    Aye me, aye me,
Shee wounds them that admire it,
Shee kils them that desire it.
    Give her pride but fuell,
    No fire is more cruell.

Pittie from ev'ry heart is fled,
    Aye me, aye me,
Since false desire could borrow
Teares of dissembled sorrow,
    Constant vowes turne truthlesse,
    Love cruell, Beauty ruthlesse.

Sorrow can laugh, and Fury sing,
    Aye me, aye me;
My raving griefes discover
I liv'd too true a lover:
    The first step to madnesse
    Is the excesse of sadnesse.

XV

Are you what your faire lookes expresse?
    O then be kinde.
From law of Nature they digresse
    Whose forme sutes not their minde:
Fairenesse seene in th'outward shape
Is but th' inward beauties Ape.

Eyes that of earth are mortall made
    What can they view?
All's but a colour or a shade,
    And neyther alwayes true.
Reasons sight, that is eterne,
Ev'n the substance can discerne.

Soule is the Man; for who will so
    The body name?
And to that power all grace we owe
    That deckes our living frame.
What, or how had housen bin,
But for them that dwell therein?

Love in the bosome is begot,
    Not in the eyes:
No beauty makes the eye more hot,
    Her flames the spright surprise:
    Let our loving mindes then meete,
    For pure meetings are most sweet.

XVII

I must complain, yet doe enjoy my Love;
She is too faire, too rich in lovely parts:
Thence is my grief, for Nature while she strove
With all her graces and divinest Arts
    To form her too too beautifull of hue,
    Shee had no leasure left to make her true.

Should I, agriev'd, then wish shee were lesse fayre?
That were repugnant to mine owne desires:
Shee is admir'd, new lovers still repayre;
That kindles daily loves forgetfull fires.
    Rest, jealous thoughts, and thus resolve at last,
    Shee hath more beauty than becomes the chast.

XVIII

Think'st thou to seduce me then with words that have no meaning?
Parats so can learne to prate, our speech by pieces gleaning:
Nurces teach their children so, about the time of weaning.

Learne to speake first, then to wooe: to wooing much pertayneth:
Hee that courts us, wanting Arte, soon falters when he fayneth,
Lookes a-squint on his discourse, and smiles when hee complaineth.

Skilfull Anglers hide their hookes, fit baytes for every season;
But with crooked pins fish thou, as babes doe that want reason;
Gogians onely can be caught with such poore trickes of treason.

Ruth forgive me if I err'd from humane hearts compassion,
When I laught sometimes too much to see thy foolish fashion:
But alas, who lesse could doe that found so good occasion!

XIX

Her fayre inflaming eyes,
    Chiefe authors of my cares,

I prai'd in humblest wise
  With grace to view my teares:
    They beheld me broad awake,
    But alasse, no ruth would take.

Her lips with kisses rich,
  And words of fayre delight,
I fayrely did beseech
  To pitty my sad plight:
    But a voyce from them brake forth
    As a whirle-winde from the North.

Then to her hands I fled,
  That can give heart and all;
To them I long did plead,
  And loud for pitty call:
    But alas, they put mee off,
    With a touch worse than a scoffe.

So backe I straight return'd,
  And at her breast I knock'd;
Where long in vaine I mourn'd,
  Her heart so fast was lock'd:
    Not a word could passage finde,
    For a Rocke inclos'd her minde.

Then downe my pray'rs made way
  To those most comely parts,
That make her flye or stay,
  As they affect deserts:
    But her angry feete, thus mov'd,
    Fled with all the parts I lov'd.

Yet fled they not so fast
  As her enraged minde:
Still did I after haste,
  Still was I left behinde,
    Till I found 'twas to no end,
    With a Spirit to contend.

XX

Turne all thy thoughts to eyes,
Turne all thy haires to eares,
Change all thy friends to spies,
And all thy joyes to feares:
>   True Love will yet be free,
>   In spite of Jealousie.

Turne darknesse into day,
Conjectures into truth,
Beleeve what th' envious say,
Let age interpret youth:
>   True love will yet be free,
>   In spite of Jealousie.

Wrest every word and looke,
Racke ev'ry hidden thought,
Or fish with golden hooke,
True love cannot be caught:
>   For that will still be free,
>   In spite of Jealousie.

XXI

If any hath the heart to kill,
>   Come rid me of this woefull paine:
For while I live I suffer still
>   This cruell torment all in vaine.
Yet none alive but one can guesse
What is the cause of my distresse.

Thanks be to heav'n, no grievous smart,
>   No maladies my limbes annoy;
I beare a sound and sprightfull heart,
>   Yet live I quite depriv'd of joy:
Since what I had, in vaine I crave,
And what I had not now I have.

A Love I had so fayre, so sweet,
>   As ever wanton eye did see:
Once by appointment wee did meet;
>   Shee would, but ah it would not be:

She gave her heart, her hand shee gave,
All did I give, shee nought could have.

What Hagge did then my powers forespeake,
   That never yet such taint did feele?
Now shee rejects me as one weake,
   Yet am I all compos'd of steele.
Ah, this is it my heart doth grieve:
Now though shee sees shee'le not believe!

XXII

Beauty, since you so much desire
To know the place of *Cupids* fire:
About you somewhere doth it rest,
Yet never harbour'd in your brest,
Nor gout-like in your heele or toe;
What foole would seeke Loves flame so low?
But a little higher, but a little higher,
There, there, o there lyes *Cupids* fire.

Thinke not, when *Cupid* most you scorne,
Men judge that you of Ice were borne:
For though you cast love at your heele,
His fury yet sometime you feele;
And where-abouts if you would know,
I tell you still not in your toe:
But a little higher, but a little higher,
There, there, o there lyes *Cupids* fire.

XXIV

Faine would I wed a faire young man, that day and night could
                                                      please mee:
When my mind or body grieved, that had the powre to ease mee.
Maids are full of longing thoughts, that breed a bloudlesse
                                                      sickenesse:
And that, oft I heare men say, is onely cur'd by quicknesse.
Oft I have been woo'd and prai'd, but never could be moved:
Many for a day or so I have most dearely loved;
But this foolish mind of mine straight loaths the thing resolved.
If to love be sinne in mee, that sinne is soone absolved.
Sure I thinke I shall at last flye to some holy Order;

When I once am setled there, then can I flye no farther.
Yet I would not dye a maid, because I had a mother:
As I was by one brought forth I would bring forth another.

From 'Poems and Sonets of Sundry Other Noblemen and
Gentlemen' appended to Newman's edition of Sidney's
Astrophel and Stella (1591)
— Campion's contributions signed 'Content' —

Canto Primo

Harke all you ladies that doo sleepe,
The fairie queene Proserpina
Bids you awake, and pitie them that weepe:
    You may doo in the darke
  What the day doth forbid;
    Feare not the doggs that barke,
      Night will have all hid.

But if you let your lovers mone,
The Fairie Queene Proserpina
Will send abroad hir Faeries ev'rie one:
    That shall pinch blacke and blew
  Your white hands and faire armes,
    That did not kindly rewe
      Your Paramours harmes.

In myrtle arbours on the downes,
The Fairie Queene Proserpina
This night by Moone shine leading merrie rounds,
    Holds a watch with sweete Love,
  Downe the dale, up the hill,
    No plaints nor grieves may move
      Their holy vigill.

All you that will hold watch with Love,
The Fairie Queene Proserpina
Will make you fairer than Dianas Dove;
    Roses red, Lillies white,
  And the cleere damaske hue
    Shall on your cheekes alight:
      Love will adorne you.

All you that love, or lov'd before,
The Fairie Queene Proserpina

    Bids you increase that loving humour more:
        They that have not yet fed
      On delight amorous,
          She vowes that they shall lead
            Apes in Avernus.

Canto Secundo

    What faire pompe have I spide of glittering Ladies,
    With locks sparckled abroad, and rosie Coronet
    On their yvorie browes, trackt to the daintie thies
    With roabs like *Amazons*, blew as Violet:
    With gold Aglets adornd, some in a changeable
    Pale, with spangs wavering taught to be moveable.

    Then those Knights that a farre off with dolorous viewing
    Cast their eyes hetherward: loe, in an agonie,
    All unbrac'd, crie aloud, their heavie state ruing;
    Moyst cheekes with blubbering painted as *Ebonie*
    Blacke, their feltred haire torne with wrathfull hand,
    And whiles astonied, starke in a maze they stand.

    But hearke what merry sound! what sodaine harmonie!
    Looke, looke neere the grove where the Ladies doe tread
    With their knights the measures waide by the melodie,
    Wantons whose travesing make men enamoured;
    Now they faine an honor, now by the slender wast
    He must lift hir aloft, and seale a kisse in hast.

    Streight downe under a shadow for wearines they lie,
    With pleasant daliance, hand knit with arme in arme,
    Now close, now set aloof they gaze with an equall eie,
    Changing kisses alike; streight with a false alarme,
    Mocking kisses alike, powt with a lovely lip.
    Thus drownd with jollities, their merry daies doe slip.

    But stay! now I discerne they goe on a Pilgrimage
    Towards Loves holy land, faire *Paphos* or *Cyprus*.
    Such devotion is meete for a blithesome age;
    With sweet youth it agrees well to be amorous.
    Let olde angrie fathers lurke in an Hermitage:
    Come, weele associate this jollie Pilgrimage!

Canto Tertio

My Love bound me with a kisse
   That I should no longer staie;
When I felt so sweete a blisse,
   I had lesse power to passe away:
Alas, that women do not knowe,
Kisses make men loath to goe.

Canto Quarto

Love whets the dullest wittes, his plagues be such,
But makes the wise by pleasing doat as much.
So wit is purchast by this dire disease:
O let me doat, so Love be bent to please.

Canto Quinto

A daie, a night, an houre of sweete content
Is worth a world consum'd in fretfull care.
Unequall Gods, in your Arbitrement
To sort us daies whose sorrowes endles are!
   And yet what were it? as a fading flower,
   To swim in blisse a daie, a night, an hower.

What plague is greater than the griefe of minde?
The griefe of minde that eates in everie vaine,
In everie vaine that leaves such clods behind,
Such clods behind as breed such bitter paine,
   So bitter paine that none shall ever finde
   What plague is greater than the griefe of minde.

Doth sorrowe fret thy soule? o direfull spirit!
Doth pleasure feede thy heart? o blessed man!
Hast thou bin happie once? o heavie plight!
Are thy mishaps forepast? o happie than!
   Or hast thou blisse in eld? o blisse too late!
   But hast thou blisse in youth? o sweete estate!

From *Observations in the Art of English Poesie* (1602)

The first Chapter, intreating of numbers in generall.

There is no writing too breefe, that without obscuritie comprehends the intent of the writer. These my late observations in English Poesy I have thus briefely gathered, that they might prove the lesse troublesome in perusing, and the more apt to be retayn'd in memorie. And I will first generally handle the nature of Numbers . . . . when we speake of a Poeme written in number, we consider not only the distinct number of the sillables, but also their value, which is contained in the length or shortnes of their sound. As in Musick we do not say a straine of so many notes, but so many sem'briefes . . . , so in a verse the numeration of the sillables is not so much to be observed, as their waite, and due proportion. In joyning of words to harmony there is nothing more offensive to the eare than to place a long sillable with a short note, or a short sillable with a long note, though in the last the vowell often beares it out. The world is made by Simmetry and proportion, and is in that respect compared to Musick, and Musick to Poetry. . . . What musick can there be where there is no proportion observed? Learning first flourished in *Greece*, from thence it was derived unto the *Romaines*, both diligent observers of the number, and quantity of sillables, not in their verses only, but likewise in their prose. Learning after the declining of the *Romaine* Empire, and the pollution of their language through the conquest of the *Barbarians*, lay most pitifully deformed, till the time of *Erasmus, Rewcline*, Sir *Thomas More*, and other learned men of that age, who brought the Latine toong againe to light, redeeming it with much labour out of the hands of the illiterate Monks and Friers. . . . In those lack-learning times, and in barbarized *Italy*, began that vulgar and easie kind of Poesie which is now in use throughout most parts of Christendome, which we abusively call Rime, and Meeter, or *Rithmus* and *Metrum*, of which I will now discourse.

The second Chapter, declaring the unaptnesse of Rime in Poesie.

I am not ignorant that whosoever shall by way of reprehension examine the imperfections of Rime, must encounter with many glorious enemies, and those very expert, and ready at their weapon, that can if neede be extempore (as they say) rime a man to death. Besides there is growne a kind of prescription in the use of Rime, to forestall the right of true numbers, as also the consent of many nations, against all which it may seeme a thing almost impossible, and vaine, to contend. All this and more can not yet deterre me from a lawful defence of perfection, or make me any whit the sooner adheare to that which is lame and unbeseeming. For custome, I alleage that ill uses are to be abolisht, and that things naturally imperfect can not be perfected by use. Old customes, if they be better, why should they not be recald, as the yet florishing custome of numerous poesy used among the *Romanes* and *Grecians*? But the unaptnes of our toongs, and the difficultie of imitation dishartens us; againe, the facilitie and popularitie of Rime creates as many Poets, as a hot sommer flies. But let me now examine the nature of that which we call Rime. By Rime is understoode that which ends in the like sound . . . The eare is a rationall sence, and a chiefe judge of proportion, but in our kind of riming what proportion is there kept, where there remaines such a confusd inequalitie of sillables? *Iambick* and *Trochaick* feete, which are opposd by nature, are by all Rimers confounded; nay, oftentimes they place instead of an *Iambick* the foot *Pyrrychius*, consisting of two short sillables, curtalling their verse, which they supply in reading with a ridiculous and unapt drawing of their speech. As for example:

Was it my desteny, or dismall chaunce?

In this verse the two last sillables of the word *Desteny*, being both short, and standing for a whole foote in the verse, cause the line to fall out shorter than it ought by nature . . . . But there is yet another fault in Rime altogether intollerable, which is, that it inforceth a man oftentimes to abjure his matter, and extend a short conceit beyond all bounds of arte: for in *Quatorzens* [fourteen-line sonnets] me thinks the Poet handles his subject as tyrannically as *Procrustes* the thiefe his prisoners, whom when he had taken, he used to cast upon a bed, which if they were too short to fill, he would stretch them longer, if too long, he would cut them shorter. Bring before me now any the most selfe-lov'd Rimer, and let me see if without blushing he be able to reade his lame halting rimes. Is there not a curse of Nature laid upon such rude Poesie, when the Writer is himself asham'd of it, and the hearers in contempt call it Riming and Ballating? What Devine in his Sermon, or grave Counseller in his Oration, will alleage the testimonie of a rime? But the devinity of the *Romaines* and *Gretians* was all written in verse: and *Aristotle*, *Galene*, and the bookes of all the excellent Philosophers are full of the testimonies of the old Poets. By them was laid the foundation of all humane wisedome, and from them the knowledge of all antiquitie is derived. I will propound but one question, and so conclude this point. If the *Italians, Frenchmen* and *Spanyards*, that with commendation have written in Rime, were demaunded whether they had rather the bookes they have publisht (if their toong would bear it) should remaine as they are in Rime, or be translated into the aunciental numbers of the *Greekes* and *Romaines*, would they not answere into numbers? What honour were it then for our English language to be the first that after so many yeares of barbarisme could second the perfection of the industrious *Greekes* and *Romaines*? which how it may be effected I will now proceede to demonstrate.

The third Chapter: of our English numbers in generall.

There are but three feete, which generally distinguish the Greeke and Latine verses, the *Dactil*, consisting of one long sillable and two short, as $v\bar{\imath}v\breve{e}r\breve{e}$; the *Trochy*, of one long and one short, as $v\bar{\imath}t\breve{a}$; and the *Iambick* of one short and one long, as $\breve{a}m\bar{o}r$. The *Spondee* of two long, the *Tribrach* of three short, the *Anapaestick* of two short and a long, are but as servants to the first. Divers other feete I know are by the Grammarians cited, but to little purpose. The *Heroical* verse that is distinguisht by the *Dactile* hath bene oftentimes attempted in our English toong, but with passing pitifull successe: and no wonder, seeing it is an attempt altogether against the nature of our language. For both the concurse of our monasillables make our verses unapt to slide [to flow], and also if we examine our polysillables, we shall find few of them by reason of their heavinesse, willing to serve in place of a *Dactile*. Thence it is, that the writers of English heroicks do so often repeate *Amyntas, Olympus, Avernus, Erinnis,* and such like borrowed words, to supply the defect of our hardly intreated *Dactile*. I could in this place set downe many ridiculous kinds of *Dactils* which they use, but that is not my purpose here to incite men to laughter. If we therefore reject the *Dactil* as unfit for our use (which of necessity we are enforst to do), there remayne only the *Iambick* foote, of which the *Iambick* verse is fram'd, and the *Trochee*, from which the *Trochaick* numbers have their originall. Let us now then examine the property of these two feete, and try if they consent with the nature of English sillables. And first for the *Iambicks*, they fall out so naturally in our toong, that, if we examine our owne writers, we shall find they unawares hit oftentimes upon the true *Iambick* numbers, but alwayes ayme at them as far as their eare without the guidance of arte can attain unto, as it shall hereafter more evidently appeare. The *Trochaick* foote, which is but an *Iambick* turn'd over and over, must of force in like manner accord in proportion with our British sillables, and so produce an English *Trochaicall* verse. Then having these two principall kinds of verses, we may easily out of them derive other formes, as the Latines and Greekes before us have done, whereof I will make plaine demonstration, beginning at the *Iambick* verse.

The fourth Chapter, of the Iambick verse.

I have observed, and so may any one that is either practis'd in singing, or hath a naturall eare able to time a song, that the Latine verses of sixe feete, as the *Heroick* and *Iambick*, or of five feete, as the *Trochaick*, are in nature all of the same length of sound with our English verses of five feete; for either of them being tim'd with the hand, . . . they fill up the quantity (as it were) of five sem'briefs; as for example, if any man will prove to time these verses with his hand.

A pure *Iambick*.
Suis et ipsa Roma viribus ruit.

A licentiate *Iambick*.
Ducunt volentes fata, nolentes trahunt.

An *Heroick* verse.
Tytere, tu patulae recubans sub tegmine fagi.

A *Trochaick* verse.
Nox est perpetua una dormienda.

English *Iambicks* pure.
The more secure, the more the stroke we feele
Of unprevented harms; so gloomy stormes
Appeare the sterner if the day be cleere.

Th' English *Iambick* licentiate.
Harke how these winds do murmur at thy flight.

The English *Trochee*.
Still where Envy leaves, remorse doth enter.

The cause why these verses differing in feete yeeld the same length of sound, is by reason of some rests which either the necessity of the numbers or the heavines of the sillables do beget. For we find in musick that oftentimes the straines of a song cannot be reduct to true number without some rests prefixt in the beginning and middle, as also at the close if need requires. Besides, our English monasillables enforce many breathings which no doubt greatly lengthen a verse, so that it is no wonder if for these reasons our English verses of five feete hold pace with the *Latines* of sixe. The pure *Iambick* in English needes small demonstration, because it consists simply of *Iambick* feete, but our *Iambick licentiate* offers itselfe to a farther consideration; for in the third and fift place we must of force hold the *Iambick* foote, in the first, second, and fourth place we may use a *Spondee* or *Iambick* and sometime a *Tribrack* or *Dactile*, but rarely an *Anapestick* foote, and that in the second or fourth place. But why an *Iambick* in the third place? I answere, that the forepart of the verse may the gentlier slide into his *Dimeter*, as, for example sake, devide this verse: *Harke how these winds do murmure at thy flight. Harke how these winds*, there the voice naturally affects a rest, then *murmur at thy flight*, that is of itselfe a perfect number, as I will declare in the next Chapter, and therefore the other odde sillable betweene them ought to be short, least the verse should hang too much betweene the naturall pause of the verse, and the *Dimeter* following; the which *Dimeter*, though it be naturally *Trochaical*, yet it seemes to have his originall out of the *Iambick* verse. But the better to confirme and expresse these rules, I will set downe a short Poeme in *Licentiate Iambicks*, which may give more light to them that shall hereafter imitate these numbers.

> Goe numbers, boldly passe, stay not for ayde
> Of shifting rime, that easie flatterer
> Whose witchcraft can the ruder eares beguile;
> Let your smooth feete, enur'd to purer arte,
> True measures tread; what if your pace be slow,
> And hops not like the Grecian elegies?
> It is yet gracefull, and well fits the state
> Of words ill-breathed, and not shap't to runne.
> Goe then, but slowly till your steps be firme;
> Tell them that pitty, or perversely skorne
> Poore English Poesie as the slave to rime,
> You are those loftie numbers that revive

> Triumphs of Princes, and sterne tragedies:
> And learne henceforth t' attend those happy sprights
> Whose bounding fury, height, and waight affects.
> Assist their labour, and sit close to them,
> Never to part away till for desert
> Their browes with great *Apollos* bayes are hid.
> He first taught number, and true harmonye;
> Nor is the lawrell his for rime bequeath'd.
> Call him with numerous accents paisd by arte,
> He'le turne his glory from the sunny clymes,
> The North-bred wits alone to patronise.
> Let France their *Bartas*, Italy *Tasso* prayse;
> *Phaebus* shuns none, but in their flight from him.

Though, as I said before, the naturall breathing place of our English *Iambick* verse is in the last sillable of the second foote, as our *Trochy* after the manner of the Latine *Heroick* and *Iambick* rests naturally in the first of the third foote, yet no man is tyed altogether to observe this rule, but he may alter it, after the judgment of his eare, which Poets, Orators, and Musitions of all men ought to have most excellent.... To proceede farther, I see no reason why the English *Iambick* in his first place may not as well borrow a foote of the *Trochy*, as our *Trochy* or the Latine *Hendicasillable* may in the like case make bold with the *Iambick*; but it must be done ever with this caveat, which is, that a *Sponde*, *Dactile* or *Tribrack* do supply the next place: for an *Iambick* beginning with a single short sillable, and the other ending before with the like, would too much drinke up the verse if they came immediately together.

> The example of the *Sponde* after the *Trochy*.
> As the faire sonne the lightsome heav'n adorns.

> The example of the *Dactil*.
> Noble, ingenious, and discreetly wise.

> The example of the *Tribrack*.
> Beawty to jelosie brings joy, sorrow, feare.

Though I have set downe these second licenses as good and ayreable enough, yet for the most part my first rules are generall.

These are those numbers which Nature in our English destinates to the Tragick and Heroick Poeme: for the subject of them both being all one, I see no impediment why one verse may not serve for them both....

The *Iambick* verse in like manner being yet made a little more licentiate[free], that it may thereby the neerer imitate our common talke, will excellently serve for Comedies; and then may we use a *Sponde* in the fift place, and in the third place any foote except a *Trochy*, which never enters into our *Iambick* verse but in the first place, and then with his caveat of the other feete which must of necessitie follow.

The fifth Chapter, of the Iambick Dimeter, or English march.

The *Dimeter* (so called in the former Chapter) I intend next of all to handle, because it seems to be a part of the *Iambick*, which is our most naturall and auncient English verse. We may terme this our English march, because the verse answers our warlick forme of march in similitude of number. But call it what you please, for I will not wrangle about names, only intending to set down the nature of it and true structure. It consists of two feete and one odde sillable. The first foote may be made either a *Trochy*, or a *Spondee*, or an *Iambick*, at the pleasure of the composer, though most naturally that place affects a *Trochy* or *Spondee*; yet, by the example of *Catullus* in his *Hendicasillables*, I adde in the first place sometimes an *Iambick* foote. In the second place we must ever insert a *Trochy* or *Tribrack*, and so leave the last sillable (as in the end of a verse it is alwaies held) common. Of this kinde I will subscribe three examples, the first being a peece of a *Chorus* in a Tragedy.

>   Raving warre begot
>   In the thirstye sands
>   Of the *Lybian* Iles
>   Wasts our emptye fields;
>   What the greedye rage
>   Of fell wintrye stormes
>   Could not turne to spoile,
>   Fierce *Bellona* now
>   Hath laid desolate,
>   Voyd of fruit, or hope.
>   Th'eger thriftye hinde
>   Whose rude toyle reviv'd

>Our skie-blasted earth
>Himselfe is but earth,
>Left a skorne to fate
>Through seditious armes:
>And that soile, alive
>Which he duly nurst,
>Which him duly fed,
>Dead his body feeds:
>Yet not all the glebe
>His tuffe hands manur'd
>Now one turfe affords
>His poor funerall.
>Thus still needy lives,
>Thus still needy dyes
>Th' unknowne multitude.

* * *

The sixt Chapter: of the English Trochaick verse.

Next in course to be intreated of is the English *Trochaick*, being a verse simple, and of it selfe depending. It consists, as the Latine *Trochaick*, of five feete, the first whereof may be a *Trochy*, a *Spondee*, or an *Iambick*, the other foure of necessity all *Trochyes*, still holding this rule authenticall, that the last sillable of a verse is alwayes common. The spirit of this verse most of all delights in *Epigrams*, but it may be diversly used, as shall hereafter be declared. I have written divers light Poems in this kinde, which for the better satisfaction of the reader, I thought convenient here in way of example to publish. In which though sometimes under a knowne name I have shadowed a fain'd conceit, yet it is done without reference, or offence to any person, and only to make the stile appeare the more English.

>The first *Epigramme*.
>Lockly spits apace, the rhewme he cals it,
>But no drop (though often urgd) he straineth
>From his thirstie jawes, yet all the morning
>And all day he spits, in ev'ry corner;
>At his meales he spits, at ev'ry meeting,
>At the barre he spits before the Fathers,
>In the Court he spits before the Graces,
>In the Church he spits, thus all prophaning

With that rude disease, that empty spitting:
Yet no cost he spares, he sees the Doctors,
Keepes a strickt diet, precisely useth
Drinks and bathes drying, yet all prevailes not.
'Tis not *China (Lockly)*, *Salsa Guacum*,
Nor dry *Sassafras* can help, or ease thee;
'Tis no humor hurts, it is thy humor.

* * *

The third *Epigramme*.
Kate can fancy only berdles husbands,
Thats the cause she shakes off ev'ry suter,
Thats the cause she lives so stale a virgin,
For, before her heart can heate her answer,
Her smooth youths she finds all hugely berded.

* * *

The seaventh Chapter, of the English Elegeick *verse.*

The *Elegeick* verses challenge the next place, as being of all compound verses the simplest. They are deriv'd out of our owne naturall numbers as neere the imitation of the *Greekes* and *Latines* as our heavy sillables will permit. The first verse is a meere licentiate *Iambick*; the second is fram'd of two united *Dimeters*. In the first *Dimeter* we are tyed to make the first foote either a *Trochy* or a *Spondee*, the second a *Trochy*, and the odde sillable of it alwaies long. The second *Dimeter* consists of two *Trochyes* (because it requires more swiftnes than the first) and an odde sillable, which being last, is ever common. I will give you example both of *Elegye* and *Epigramme*, in this kinde.

An *Elegye*.
Constant to none, but ever false to me,
    Traiter still to love through thy faint desires,
Not hope of pittie now nor vaine redresse
    Turns my griefs to teares, and renu'd laments.
Too well thy empty vowes, and hollow thoughts
    Witnes both thy wrongs, and remorseles hart.
Rue not my sorrow, but blush at my name,

    Let thy bloudy cheeks guilty thoughts betray.
My flames did truly burne, thine made a shew,
    As fires painted are which no heate retayne,
Or as the glossy *Pirop* faines to blaze,
    But, toucht, cold appeares, and an earthy stone.
True cullours deck thy cheeks, false foiles thy brest,
    Frailer than thy light beawty is thy minde.
None canst thou long refuse, nor long affect,
    But turn'st feare with hopes, sorrow with delight,
Delaying, and deluding ev'ry way
    Those whose eyes are once with thy beawty chain'd.
Thrice happy man that entring first thy love
    Can so guide the straight raynes of his desires,
That both he can regard thee, and refraine:
    If grac't, firme he stands, if not, easely falls.

       Example of *Epigrams*, in *Elegeick* verse.
         *   *   *

          The fourth *Epigramme*.
A wiseman wary lives, yet most secure,
    Sorrowes move not him greatly, nor delights:
Fortune and death he skorning, only makes
    Th' earth his sober Inne; but still heav'n his home.
         *   *   *
          The sixt *Epigramme*.
Drue gives thee money, yet thou thankst not him,
    But thankst God for him, like a godly man.
Suppose, rude Puritan, thou begst of him,
    And he saith God help, who's the godly man?

          The seventh *Epigramme*.
All wonders *Barnzy* speakes, all grosely faind,
    Speake some wonder once, *Barnzy,* speake the truth.

     *   *   *

      The eight Chapter: of Ditties *and* Odes.

To descend orderly from the more simple numbers to them that are more compounded, it is now time to handle such verses as are fit for *Ditties* or *Odes*; which we may call *Lyricall*, because they are apt to be soong to an instrument, if they were adorn'd with convenient notes. Of that kind I will demonstrate three in this Chapter, and in the first we will proceede after the manner of the *Saphick* which is a *Trochaicall* verse as well as the *Hendicasillable* in Latine. The first three verses therefore in our English *Saphick* are meerely those *Trochaicks* which I handled in the sixt Chapter, excepting only that the first foote of either of them must ever of necessity be a *Spondee*, to make the number more grave. The fourth and last closing verse is compounded of three *Trochyes* together, to give a more smooth farewell, as you may easily observe in this Poeme made upon a Triumph at *Whitehall*, whose glory was dasht with an unwelcome showre, hindring the people from the desired sight of her Majestie.

The English *Sapphick*.

Faiths pure shield, the Christian *Diana*,
Englands glory crownd with all devinenesse,
Live long with triumphs to blesse thy people
    At thy sight triumphing.

Loe, they sound, the Knights in order armed
Entring threat the list, adrest to combat
For their courtly loves; he, hees the wonder
    Whome *Eliza* graceth.

Their plum'd pomp the vulgar heaps detaineth,
And rough steeds; let us the still devices
Close observe, the speeches and the musicks
    Peacefull arms adorning.

But whence showres so fast this angry tempest,
Clowding dimme the place? Behold *Eliza*
This day shines not here; this heard, the launces
    And thick heads do vanish.

The second kinde consists of *Dimeter*, whose first foote may either be a *Sponde* or a *Trochy*. The two verses following are both of them *Trochaical*, and consist of foure feete, the first of either of them being a *Spondee* or *Trochy*, the other three only *Trochyes*. The fourth and last verse is made of two *Trochyes*. The number is voluble, and fit to expresse any amorous conceit.

The Example.

Rose-cheekt *Lawra*, come
Sing thou smoothly with thy beawties
Silent musick, either other
    Sweetely gracing.

Lovely formes do flowe
From concent devinely framed,
Heav'n is musick, and thy beawties
    Birth is heavenly.

These dull notes we sing
Discords neede for helps to grace them;
Only beawty purely loving
    Knowes no discord:

But still mooves delight
Like cleare springs renu'd by flowing,
Ever perfet, ever in them-
    selves eternall.

The third kind begins as the second kind ended, with a verse consisting of two *Trochy* feete, and then as the second kind had in the middle two *Trochaick* verses of foure feete, so this hath three of the same nature, and ends in a *Dimeter* as the second began. The *Dimeter* may allow in the first place a *Trochy* or a *Spondee*, but no *Iambick*.

The Example.

Just beguiler,
Kindest love, yet only chastest,
Royall in thy smooth denyals,
Frowning or demurely smiling
    Still my pure delight.

Let me view thee
With thoughts and with eyes affected,
And if then the flames do murmur,
Quench them with thy vertue, charme them
    With thy stormy browes.

> Heav'n so cheerefull
> Laughs not ever, hory winter
> Knowes his season, even the freshest
> Sommer mornes from angry thunder
> Jet not still secure.

The ninth Chapter, of the Anacreontick Verse.

If any shall demaund the reason why this number, being it selfe simple, is plac't after so many compounded numbers, I answere, because I hold it a number too licentiate for a higher place, and in respect of the rest imperfect; yet is it passing gracefull in our English toong, and will excellently fit the subject of a *Madrigall*, or any other lofty or tragicall matter. It consists of two feete: the first may be either a *Sponde* or *Trochy*, the other must ever represent the nature of a *Trochy*, as for example:

> Follow, followe
> Though with mischiefe
> Arm'd, like whirlewind
> Now she flyes thee;
> Time can conquer
> Loves unkindnes;
> Love can alter
> Times disgraces;
> Till death faint not
> Then but followe.
> Could I catch that
> Nimble trayter,
> Skornefull *Lawra*,
> Swift foote *Lawra*,
> Soone then would I
> Seeke avengement.
> Whats th' avengement?
> Even submissely
> Prostrate then to
> Beg for mercye.

Thus have I briefely described eight several kinds of English numbers simple or compound. . . . These numbers which by my long observation I have found agreeable with the nature of our sillables, I have set forth for the benefit of our language, which I presume the learned will not only imitate, but also polish and amplifie with their owne inventions. Some eares accustomed altogether to the fatnes of rime, may perhaps except against the cadences of these numbers; but let any man judicially examine them, and he shall finde they close of themselves so perfectly, that the help of rime were not only in them superfluous, but also absurd. Moreover, that they agree with the nature of our English it is manifest, because they entertaine so willingly our owne British names, which the writers in English Heroicks could never aspire unto, and even our Rimers themselves have rather delighted in borrowed names than in their owne, though much more apt and necessary. ...

The tenth Chapter, of the quantity of English sillables.

The *Greekes* in the quantity of their sillables were farre more licentious than the *Latines*.... But the English may very well challenge much more licence than either of them, by reason it stands chiefely upon monasillables, which, in expressing with the voyce, are of a heavy cariage, and for that cause the *Dactil*, *Trybrack*, and *Anapestick* are not greatly mist in our verses. But above all the accent of our words is diligently to be observ'd, for chiefly by the accent in any language the true value of the sillables is to be measured. Neither can I remember any impediment except position that can alter the accent of any sillable in our English verse. For though we accent the second of *Trumpington* short, yet it is naturally long, and so of necessity must be held of every composer. Wherefore the first rule that is to be observed is the nature of the accent, which we must ever follow. ...

Also, because our English Orthography (as the French) differs from our common pronunciation, we must esteeme our sillables as we speake, not as we write, for the sound of them in a verse is to be valued, and not their letters. ...

*   *   *

[Campion concludes his elaborate dissertation 'of the quantity of English sillables' with this dictum: 'there is no Art begun and perfected at one enterprise.' *Ed.*]

NOTES

p. 26. *I ('My sweetest Lesbia let us live and love')*: based on Catullus' 'Vivamus, mea Lesbia, atque amemus', often translated by seventeenth-century poets.

p. 29. *VIII ('It fell on a sommers day')*: Campion wrote two Latin versions of this song: 'De Thermanio et Glaia' and its revision, 'In Lycium et Clytham'.

dumpe: fit of abstraction. (Used by Sidney: 'Some good old dump that Chaucers mistresse knew'.)

p. 30. *Sypres*: mourning crape.

X ('Follow your Saint, follow with accents sweet'): part of the setting for this song was used for 'Love me or not', in the *Fourth Booke*.

p. 41. *Hally*: Henry Frederick, Prince of Wales, died in 1612 aged eighteen. *Songs of Mourning*, 'worded' by Campion, appeared in 1613.

p. 42. *prove*: try the value of.

p. 43. *III ('Harden now thy tyred hart, with more than flinty rage')*: based on Catullus.

p. 45. *X ('What harvest halfe so sweet is')*: the first six lines (based on Catullus) are taken from VII in the 1601 *Booke of Ayres*.

p. 49. *stickler*: either an umpire or (more logically here) an active contender.

the starry flowre: heliotrope.

p. 52. *enlargement*: release from prison.

stand onely mute: this could be a grim reference to the 'standing mute' of Richard Weston, whose trial had opened the proceedings against Overbury's murderer's. By consenting, later, to plead guilty, Weston escaped the horrors of the *peine forte et dure*, only to be hanged instead.

p. 55. *The Grecian, inchanted all parts but the heele*: Achilles.

p. 59. *yron men*: men of the Iron (not Golden) Age.

Palme tree the more you presse, the more it growes: according to Pliny's *Natural History*.

p. 63. *The hope you wing'd*: an image from falconry.

p. 64. *the Pawne*: a street of London dress shops, built in 1571.

Astraea: the virgin goddess of the Golden Age.

p. 68. *Gogians*: gudgeon, small fish which are easy to catch.

p. 73. *rewe*: pity.

CANTVS

I.

Author of light reviue my dying spright,
Redeeme it from the snares of all con-foun-ding night.
Lord, light me to thy blessed way: For blinde, for blinde with worldly vaine desires, I wander as a stray:
Sunne and Moone, Starres and vnderlights I see,
But all their glorious beames are mists and darknesse being compar'd to thee.

1 Author of light reviue my dying spright,
Redeeme it from the snares of all-confounding night.
   Lord, light me to thy blessed way:
For blinde with worldly vaine desires I wander as a stray.
   Sunne and Moone, Starres and vnderlights I see,
But all their glorious beames are mists and darknes being compar'd to thee.

2 Fountaine of health my soules deepe wounds recure,
Sweet showres of pitty raine, wash my vncleannesse pure.
   One drop of thy desired grace
The faint and fading hart can raise, and in ioyes bosome place.
   Sinne and Death, Hell and tempting Fiends may rage;
But God his owne will guard, and their sharp paines and griefe in time asswage.

p. 74. *Aglets*: hanging dress ornaments. *Pale*: a fabric of multi-coloured stripes. *spangs*: spangles. *feltred*: felted, matted. *waide*: weighed, measured. *travesing*: movement. *honor*: bow.
p. 75. *clods*: clots.
p. 76. *Rewcline*: Johann Reuchlin (1455-1522), German humanist. *rime a man to death*: a reference to Sidney's *Defence of Poesie*.
p. 77. *... as tyrannically as Procrustes...* : Ben Jonson used this analogy in his conversations with Drummond of Hawthornden.
p. 79. *Suis et ...* : 'and through her own strength Rome is falling' (Horace, *Epode* xvi, 1. 2).
Ducunt ... : 'the fates lead the willing, and the unwilling they drag' (Seneca, *Epistle* CVII. 11).
Tytere, ... : 'you, Tityrus, lying in the shade of the spreading beech-tree' (Virgil, *Eclogue* I, 1. 1).
Nox est ... : 'we must sleep one perpetual night' (Catullus, *Carmina* V, 1. 6).
p. 81. *paisd*: weighed.
Bartas, ... Tasso: Guillaume Salluste du Bartas and Torquato Tasso, sixteenth-century epic poets.
p. 82. *common*: either long or short.
p. 84. *China ... dry Sassafras*: medicaments.
The third Epigramme: English version of the 1595 Latin epigram 'In Laurentiam'.
p. 85. *Pirop*: red bronze.
Barnzy: Campion handled Barnabe Barnes (*c.* 1569-1609) roughly in his Latin epigrams, but wrote prefatory verses for his *Foure Bookes of Offices*.
p. 88. *Jet*: parade proudly, make boastful show. (Nashe: 'Mistress Minx ... jets it ...')

CANTVS. VII.

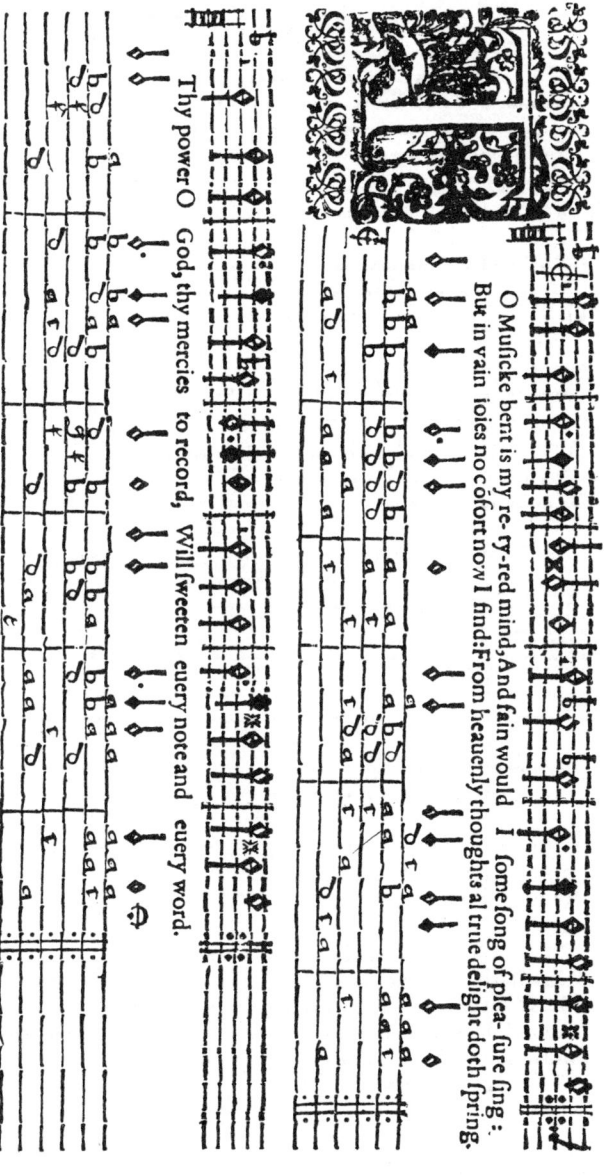

O Musicke bent is my re-ty-red mind, And fain would I some song of plea-sure sing:
But in vain ioies no cōfort now I find: From heauenly thoughts al true delight doth spring.

Thy power O God, thy mercies to record, Will sweeten euery note and euery word.

1. To Musicke bent is my retyred minde,
And faine would I some song of pleasure sing:
But in vaine ioyes no comfort now I finde:
From heau'nly thoughts all true delight doth spring.
Thy power O God, thy mercies to record
Will sweeten eu'ry note, and eu'ry word.

2. All earthly pompe or beauty to expresse,
Is but to carue in snow, on waues to write.
Celestiall things though men conceiue them lesse,
Yet fullest are they in themselues of light:
Such beames they yeeld as know no meanes to dye:
Such heate they cast as lifts the Spirit high.

INDEX OF FIRST LINES

A daie, a night, an houre of sweete content	75
All lookes be pale, harts cold as stone	41
Are you what your faire lookes expresse?	67
A secret love or two, I must confesse	50
Author of light, revive my dying spright	35
Awake, awake thou heavy spright	40
Beauty is but a painted hell	67
Beauty, since you so much desire	71
Blame not my cheeks, though pale with love they be	32
Breake now my heart and dye! Oh no, she may relent.	55
Come away, arm'd with loves delights	49
Come, chearfull day, part of my life, to mee:	40
Come, let us sound with melody the praises	32
Come, O come my lifes delight	60
Come, you pretty false-ey'd wanton	49
Ev'ry Dame affects good fame, what ere her doings be:	64
Faine would I wed a faire young man	71
Fire, fire, fire, fire!	58
Fire that must flame is with apt fuell fed	56
Followe thy faire sunne, unhappy shaddowe	27
Follow your Saint, follow with accents sweet	30
Give beauty all her right	43
Good men, shew, if you can tell	44
Harden now thy tyred hart, with more than flinty rage;	43
Harke all you ladies that doo sleepe	73
Her fayre inflaming eyes	68
I care not for these Ladies	27
If any hath the heart to kill	70
If Love loves truth, then women doe not love;	55
If thou long'st so much to learne (sweet boy) what 'tis to love	57
I must complain, yet doe enjoy my Love;	68
It fell on a sommers day	29

Kinde are her answeres	54
Loe, when backe mine eye	39
Love me or not, love her I must or dye	66
Love whets the dullest wittes, his plagues be such	75
Maydes are simple, some men say	53
Most sweet and pleasing are thy wayes, O God	38
My Love bound me with a kisse	75
My love hath vowd hee will forsake mee	28
My sweetest Lesbia let us live and love	26
Never love unlesse you can	61
Never weather-beaten Saile more willing bent to shore	39
Now winter nights enlarge	56
Oft have I sigh'd for him that heares me not:	52
O griefe, O spight, to see poore Vertue scorn'd	55
O Love, where are thy Shafts, thy Quiver and thy Bow?	66
O sweet delight, O more than humane blisse	59
O what unhop't for sweet supply!	43
Pin'd I am, and like to die	47
Respect my faith, regard my service past;	63
Seeke the Lord, and in his wayes persever!	41
See where she flies enrag'd from me	31
Shall I come, sweet Love, to thee	58
Silly boy, 'tis ful Moone yet, thy night as day shines clearely	60
Since now those clouds, that lately over-cast	52
Sleepe, angry beauty, sleep, and feare not me;	60
So quicke, so hot, so mad is thy fond sute	61
So tyr'd are all my thoughts, that sence and spirits faile;	53
Sweet, exclude mee not, nor be divided	45
That holy Hymnes with Lovers cares are knit	42
The man of life upright	35
The peacefull westerne winde	46
There is a Garden in her face	64
There is none, O none but you	47

The Sypres curten of the night is spread	30
Think'st thou to seduce me then with words	68
Thou art not faire for all thy red and white	31
Though you are yoong and I am olde	26
Though your strangenesse frets my hart	48
Thrice tosse these Oaken ashes in the ayre;	58
Thus I resolve, and time hath taught me so:	59
To Musicke bent is my retyred minde	37
Tune thy Musicke to thy hart	37
Turne all thy thoughts to eyes	70
Vaile, love, mine eyes, O hide from me	63
Vaine men whose follies make a God of Love	42
View mee, Lord, a worke of thine:	36
Were my hart as some mens are, thy errours would not move me:	53
What faire pompe have I spide of glittering Ladies	74
What harvest halfe so sweet is	45
When thou must home to shades of under ground	32
When to her lute Corrina sings	29
Where are all thy beauties now all harts enchayning?	36
Wise men patience never want	38
Young and simple though I am	65

Index of First Lines to Poems in
Observations in the Art of English Poesie

All wonders *Barnzy* speakes, all grosely faind	85
A wiseman wary lives, yet most secure	85
Constant to none, but ever false to me	84
Drue gives thee money, yet thou thankst not him	85
Faiths pure shield, the Christian *Diana*	86
Follow, followe	88
Goe numbers, boldly passe, stay not for ayde	80
Just beguiler	87
Kate can fancy only berdles husbands	84
Lockly spits apace, the rhewme he cals it	83
Raving warre begot	82
Rose-cheekt *Lawra*, come	87